INEQUALITY in SINGAPORE

Edited by

Faizal Bin Yahya
Institute of Policy Studies, Singapore

Published by

World Scientific Publishing Co. Pte. Ltd.
5 Toh Tuck Link, Singapore 596224
USA office: 27 Warren Street, Suite 401-402, Hackensack, NJ 07601
UK office: 57 Shelton Street, Covent Garden, London WC2H 9HE

British Library Cataloguing-in-Publication Data
A catalogue record for this book is available from the British Library.

INEQUALITY IN SINGAPORE

Copyright © 2015 by World Scientific Publishing Co. Pte. Ltd.

All rights reserved. This book, or parts thereof, may not be reproduced in any form or by any means, electronic or mechanical, including photocopying, recording or any information storage and retrieval system now known or to be invented, without written permission from the publisher.

For photocopying of material in this volume, please pay a copying fee through the Copyright Clearance Center, Inc., 222 Rosewood Drive, Danvers, MA 01923, USA. In this case permission to photocopy is not required from the publisher.

ISBN 978-981-4656-80-1
ISBN 978-981-4623-83-4 (pbk)

In-house Editor: Sandhya Venkatesh

Typeset by Stallion Press
Email: enquiries@stallionpress.com

Printed in Singapore

CONTENTS

Chapter 1: Introduction   1
Is Life Getting Better in Singapore?: Issues on Social Inequality
Professor Paul Cheung

Chapter 2: Inclusive Growth   13
Growing Inclusivity, Addressing Labor Market Shortfalls and Enhancing International Competitiveness
Speaker: Associate Professor Tan Khee Giap
Discussant: Mr Yeoh Lam Keong

Chapter 3: Education and Social Mobility   25
Education and Intergenerational Mobility
Speaker: Associate Professor Irene Ng
Discussant: Associate Professor Tan Ern Ser

Chapter 4: Retirement Funding and Adequacy   51
Retirement Funding Adequacy in Singapore
Speaker: Associate Professor Hui Weng Tat
Discussant: Mr Chan Beng Seng

Chapter 5: Foreign Talent and Their Impact on the Singapore Economy 77

Impact of Foreign Workers on Economic Growth of Singapore Economy
Speaker: Associate Professor Shandre M Thangavelu
Discussant: Ms Wong Su-Yen

Chapter 6: Health Care and Long-term Care 111

Health and Long-term Care for the Aging Population in Singapore
Speaker: Associate Professor Phua Kai Hong
Discussant: Ms Lim Sia Hoe

Chapter 7: Housing Affordability 133

Is Housing Still Affordable?: New Disaggregated Indicators
Speaker: Associate Professor Lum Sau Kim and Ms Zhou Xuefeng
Discussant: Mr Christopher Gee

About the Speakers 165

About the Discussants 171

Index 175

CHAPTER 1

INTRODUCTION

Is Life Getting Better in Singapore?: Issues on Social Inequality

PROFESSOR PAUL CHEUNG
Department of Social Work, National University of Singapore

1. IS LIFE GETTING BETTER IN SINGAPORE?

Singapore poses an interesting paradox in national development. As a small city-state devoid of natural resources, it has done surprisingly well. Singapore is consistently ranked in the top tier of per capita gross domestic product (GDP) and the annual average for the last few years exceeded US$50,000 per person. Its GDP has grown at an average of 6% per year in the past decade. In appearance, Singaporeans are the envy of the region, enjoying a high quality home, full employment, and efficient public infrastructure. Indeed, international quantitative development indices, such as United Nations human development index, have repeatedly ranked Singapore in the top tier.

In spite of this apparent prosperity and well-being, the average Singaporean appears to have many grievances about life in Singapore. Complaints on one issue or another are often found in letters to the local newspapers. Social media has become a popular channel for the Singaporeans to voice their unhappiness over a host of issues. Compared with similar affluent countries in the Nordic region, Singaporeans manifest a much lower level of "happiness" as reported by the 2013 World Happiness Report. Are these grievances just simple, day-to-day reactions to competitive urban life with no lasting significance? Or are they reflective of deeper anxieties and critical structural tensions in Singapore?

Dissatisfactions with municipal issues (transport, waste management, traffic, tree trimming, etc.) are part and parcel of urban life. City-dwellers have to deal with day-to-day stress arising from crowding or competition for scarce resources. There is no perfect urban system, and it is accepted that city-dwellers face far more daily hassles than their rural counterparts. Singapore is no exception and complaints arising from urban living are just part of the feedback system to make city-living better. It is widely acknowledged that the Singapore government takes municipal issues seriously, and the bureaucracy is genuinely responsive to public feedback. The quality of urban living in Singapore has been termed the "Singapore premium", denoting the competitive advantage that Singapore derives from an efficient and well-run urban system. With continuing efforts to improve its livability and urban design, this "Singapore premium" is unlikely to be diminished.

Given the apparent success of Singapore in managing its urban life and economic development, are there genuine grievances among the local population? Singaporeans are known for being quick in voicing their complaints. Are these complaints skin-deep or are they reflections of deeper structural issues? The 2011 General Election (GE) perhaps gave the clearest indication that there was real unhappiness among the local population over a host of important national issues. Initially, it was expected that the 2011 GE would be another run-of-the-mill election with municipal issues taking center stage. Such issues are easily handled with the usual government promises or minor policy adjustments. However, the intense debate leading to the GE and the final election results showed a level of discontent, yet unheard of in Singapore politics. It appears that the grievances, and the underlying anxieties that the population is feeling, have now been articulated by politicians and brought to the open. Solutions to these issues are still being debated. Judging from the reactions of the government, there seem to be initial attempts to address some of the issues.

The underlying anxieties of the average Singaporean appear to arise from the perception of financial insecurity and livelihood uncertainties, and the corresponding lack of government support. There is also growing concern on whether an average person could continue to achieve the "Singaporean dream" and whether these aspirations are being dashed by the inflow of foreigners. With rising costs of living and stagnating wages, Singaporeans are becoming alarmed by the growing income inequality. It appears that the good life that a Singaporean expects is now harder to attain. The Housing and Development Board (HDB) flat, promised to every Singaporean family, seems to be beyond reach; health care is increasingly expensive; and the flooding of foreigners into every sphere of life gives the impression that foreigners are taking away the benefits promised to Singaporeans. In a country without a universal "social welfare" system, the average Singaporean has come to feel threatened and worried about his/her future. These anxieties are compounded by the ageing of the population, and the frequent stories of older Singaporeans trapped in their own home with very little cash to live on.

The Institute of Policy Studies (IPS) of the Lee Kuan Yew School of Public Policy convened a number of seminars to explore these deeper issues in Singapore society today, particularly those that were voiced at the 2011 GE and by concerned researchers. In 2012, the Singapore Perspectives Conference carried the title of "Singapore Inclusive: Bridging Divides", which addressed the issues of income inequality and its ramifications. Subsequently, additional seminars were held. This book is a representation of the key issues being discussed through a collection of articles focusing on five key areas of social concern. A brief introduction to each area is given below.

2. CRITICAL SOCIAL ISSUES AND PUBLIC CONCERNS

2.1. Wage Stagnation and Competition of Foreigners

A key issue that has attracted much attention in the past decade is the rising income inequality. The steady rise of the Gini coefficient, from 0.442 in 2000 to 0.478 in 2012, has been widely noted. Indeed, the United Nations human development report has ranked Singapore as the second highest in income inequality among the "high development countries". This increase in the Gini coefficient is consistent with other indicators of rising inequality. For example, the share of national wage incomes for the lower 50% households has steadily declined over time. The income ratio of the top 20% of the working population versus the bottom 20% has correspondingly risen over time.

The rise in income inequality has been argued (and accepted) as somewhat inevitable as Singapore develops into a financial, high technology, and trading hub. For those with the skill and education, there are plenty of high-paying jobs among local and foreign firms. Income inequality, just like inflation, may be deemed as a necessary driver for economic expansion and development, as long as it does not give rise to social tension. Singaporeans seem to have accepted this narrative of the inevitability of income inequality as it is consistent with the government ideology of meritocracy and market-determined compensation. Other developed countries show similar trends, with the benefits of economic expansion increasingly concentrated among the top 10% of the working population. This growing gap between the top and the bottom is attracting global attention, and concerns of the disappearing middle class have been voiced. In response, the call for progressive taxes and an enhanced social welfare system is getting louder.

In Singapore, the data clearly shows that not all have benefitted from economic expansion in the past decade. Hui Weng Tat, in this volume, has argued that

> *"aggregate wage share has fallen; wages are stagnating at the lower end of the income ladder, the share of total incomes has fallen for the majority of households; the unemployment rate has climbed to a higher average level in the past decade; a rapidly ageing labor force has led to older workers shouldering a dominant share of total employment."*

The chart below, used by Hui and others, shows the gross monthly income by deciles and it is clear that wage increases have been marginal for the lower deciles.

Employed Residents (excluding NSFs) aged fifteen years and over by Gross Monthly Income from Work (excluding Employer CPF)

Year	10th	20th	30th	40th	50th	80th	90th Percentile
2002	926				2401	4478	6436
2003	876				2371	4468	6459
2004	881				2333	4422	6427
2006	819				2358	4695	6754
2007a	837				2429	4887	7207
2008	829				2486	5069	7596
2009	826				2467	4973	7385
2010	828				2486	5077	7591
2011	820				2497	5134	7729
2012	791				2524	5111	7714

SGD$ (at 2009 prices)

Source: *Labour Force in Singapore 2012*, Ministry of Manpower, Singapore

Researchers have also focused on the emergence of the "working poor" among the Singapore workforce: those who are gainfully employed but their wage level is too low to cover basic expenses. Indeed, the non-governmental sector has begun concerted efforts to raise public awareness on the prevalence of urban poverty in affluent Singapore. The "partnership against poverty" initiated by Caritas has attracted much attention through its innovative social media advertisements. The BBC's story on the hidden poverty in Singapore was widely viewed.

No data is available to pin down the size and characteristics of the "working poor" population, nor the impact of this growing income inequality on household budgets and well-being. The government has so far been reluctant to share data to enable independent research on these issues. Data available in the public domain seems to suggest that this population tends to concentrate in the services sector and the workers are older in age. The "working poor" are likely to be in jobs that can be easily taken up by foreign workers. Feedbacks from social service professionals have voiced humanitarian concerns among some of the affected families.

Discussions on the "working poor" and rising income inequality have led to a number of policy suggestions. To address the issue of stagnating wage level, Professor Lim Chong Yah has recommended in 2012, somewhat offhandedly, a quick wage adjustment policy for low-wage workers, raising the wage level by 15% in the first year, a further 15% in the second, and 20% in the third. The National Trade Union Council (NTUC) has since recommended a Progressive Wage Model (PWM) with structured wage increases through career progression and increased productivity. In addition, calls for a minimum wage have been made among researchers and the general public. While the government has steadfastly refused to implement an across-the-board minimum wage scheme, it has accepted a proposal from NTUC to impose a starting wage of S$1000 for the cleaning sector. It is likely that such sector-specific minimum wage schemes will be extended and expanded in the future.

The stagnation in wage level in the local workforce has been attributed by researchers to the ease of recruitment of foreign workers and the persistence of low productivity in some sectors. The impact of the easy availability of foreign workers in Singapore's labor market has been an intense topic of public discussion. In this volume, Tan Khee Giap's paper "Growing Inclusivity, Addressing Labor Market Shortfalls and Enhancing International Competitiveness", addresses this key issue of the wage-productivity nexus and how to move part of the workforce from low wage-low productivity to high wage-high productivity. He argues for the need to enhance skill-matching, skill-upgrading, and comprehensive educational investment for the local workforce. In addition, he argues for the need to rationalize the inflow of foreign workers. In his comments, Yeoh Lam Keong reiterates the need to restrict labor supply through tight control of foreign workforce and argues that the wages for some sectors have been "artificially depressed for over two decades".

Shandre Thangavelu's paper "Impact of Foreign Workers on Economic Growth of Singapore Economy", examines further the impact of foreign workers by assessing the relative productivity of local versus foreign workers. He shares the view that greater inflow of low-skilled foreign workers could dampen Singapore's productivity growth and export competitiveness. In her comments, Wong Su Yen argues that the free flow of talents is important for future growth, given Singapore's low unemployment rate and hub-based economy. She cautions that this must be balanced against the perception of government policies that seem to be too pro-foreigner and there is a need to address unemployability and skill gaps.

The debate on how to reduce income inequality through invigorating wage growth at the lower end of the income distribution, will no doubt continue. Restricting supply of foreign workforce could be one of the solutions as this would push up the wages of local workforce. Unless matched by improving productivity, high wages across the board could also hurt Singapore's economic competitiveness. NTUC's PWM could be an interesting experiment and if successful, it could help enhance the income growth of those in the low-wage sectors. In the meantime, the initiation of a process toward a national minimum wage may reassure Singaporeans that the government will take the necessary steps to enhance the well-being of low-wage workers.

2.2. Barriers to Upward Mobility

An important feature of the social contract between the government and Singaporeans is that there should be no barrier to upward mobility. The Prime Minister, in his 2013 National Day Rally speech, has reaffirmed that the government will do more to keep paths upwards open to all, and

> "to keep the society mobile, to bring every child to a good starting point and make sure that whichever family you are born into, whether privileged or not privileged, you are never shut out from the system and especially through education."

The fact that he needs to reassure the population once again, after 50 years of nation-building, that upward mobility is sacrosanct, interesting, and presumably a reaction to the growing perception that upward mobility is blocked by those from privileged backgrounds or by well-educated foreign talents.

Is the "Singapore dream" dead? Tan Ern Ser argues that the "Singapore dream has increasingly come under serious threat in the forms of economic fluctuations, global competition, cost inflation, and an ageing population, which lead to income inequality, employment and income security, higher cost of living, and high age-related support ratios." A consequence of the reduced upward mobility is the "hardening of class boundaries" which further dampens upward mobility.

The negative reaction to foreigners taking good jobs away from Singaporeans is particularly strong and well-articulated. From closed door dialogues to social media blogs, there is an abundance of anecdotes on the displacement and discrimination of locals. It is surprising that the government has never publicly acknowledged this growing negative sentiment despite its prevalence and emotional intensity. The pressure on the government to give locals some "home-court" advantage may have yielded initial results. The fair consideration framework could well be the start of a process, whereby locals are given some protection from overseas competition.

In her paper "Education and Intergenerational Mobility", Irene Ng argues that some characteristics in our school system tend to decrease intergenerational mobility. These characteristics include school-based segregation through streaming, and increasing costs of education due to corporatization. She argues for a re-think of the educational system to promote greater mobility and equal opportunities for all. In his comments, Tan Ern Ser observes that social class origin "does to some extent, even significantly, determine class destiny", and mobility chances decline further down the social ladder.

Singapore has built its success over the past 50 years on the ideology of meritocracy and upward mobility. Over time, social class boundaries may have hardened, and the segregation of the rich and the poor become more visible. But as reflected in Prime Minister's 2013 speech, the government is taking this issue seriously and has introduced some measures. It remains to be seen if the public accepts the solutions put forward by the government, and whether social class tensions will give rise to more social conflicts.

2.3. Retirement and Income Vulnerability

It is a well-known fact that Singapore is one of the fastest ageing populations globally on account of the cohorts of baby-boomers reaching age 65 in the coming years. This is a huge group, and its movement in time has had significant impact on Singapore's development. As this group ages, concerns have been raised as to whether this group is financially secured for their old age. Ageing issues have surfaced in the past, especially those concerning the destitute immigrant elderly with no family support. The current concern is different as it reflects the sentiments of a large segment of the population which has worked hard throughout their lifetime and contributed significantly to Singapore's development.

The government has put in place the Central Provident Fund (CPF), which enforces a universal save-as-you-earn scheme. This is the cornerstone for old age financial security. By all accounts, it is a successful scheme, both as a macroeconomic device to fund national development and as a means to minimize government budgetary burdens to care for the older population. However, questions have now been raised on whether the forced savings are adequate to provide for old age financial security.

Hui Weng Tat in his paper "Retirement Funding Adequacy in Singapore" addresses this concern. He argues that, for some segments of the population, spells of unemployment and housing purchases negatively impact the amount of savings available to meet an expected "income replacement rate". He is of the view that the existing CPF system is "unable to adequately provide for the retirement needs of a large majority of the resident workforce, especially the growing share of those with tertiary education in the workforce". In response, Chan Beng Seng gives a more positive assessment. Rising income across the board and increased labor force participation rates among older workers provide an added layer of financial support for the older population. To him, investment in housing is still a good fallback as such assets can be cashed in through HDB's enhanced lease buyback scheme.

The growing group of "asset rich, cash poor" among the aging population will find the academic debate on the adequacy of the CPF, irrelevant to their well-being. They face the stark choice of staying in their homes (and struggling to pay for their daily and medical expenses) or cashing in their assets and leaving the home they were promised they could age in. This clearly is not an easy choice to make. Some Singaporeans are angered by the lack of alternatives, that they are now forced to sell their beloved homes in their old age. New policy options may have to be devised to address this issue and to expand the options available. The enhanced annuity-based buy-back scheme from the HDB may be a workable alternative.

2.4. Health Care Affordability

Similar to the CPF scheme, the MediSave, MediShield, and MediFund (3M) model of health care financing is one of the major social innovations in Singapore. It has received global accolades for being efficient in pooling resources for health care and advocating individual responsibility through a co-payment scheme. The 3M model is a forced saving scheme for medical expenses but with insurance protection and a mechanism to address the needs of the very poor. However, with the rising costs of health care, and the stagnating wage income of the working class, the health care financing issue has become a serious public concern. This is a particularly sensitive issue for the aged population as their need for health care increases. The public is asking a legitimate question: Will health care be affordable at a time when it is needed?

Phua Kai Hong, Tania Ng, and Winston Chin's paper "Health and Long-term Care for the Ageing Population in Singapore" gives a comprehensive review of the issues. They acknowledge that while the co-payment scheme has helped to manage waste and overconsumption, it has led to "over-rationing" of medical resources to patients who are truly in need of them. They argue that the affordability issue has become an inhibition to the poor seeking medical treatment or rehabilitation. They also hinted that this may be related to the larger issue of stagnating wages, where the poor are no longer able to afford medical care with reduced purchasing power. Lim Sia Hoe, in his comments, argues for a dedicated eldercare framework that will address the need for medical and rehabilitative care which could build on an expanded 3M system of health care financing.

2.5. Public Housing Affordability

Like CPF and the 3M health care financing program, Singapore's public housing system has received universal acclaim as an asset-building social policy. Christopher Gee in his comments, argues that the "public housing system is one of the most powerful forces countering inequality in Singapore". There are three main benefits of public housing. Firstly, every household in Singapore is guaranteed decent housing. Secondly, public housing tenants enjoy a steady flow of financial transfers from the government, from utility rebates to facility improvement programs. Finally, with property values rising steadily over the past decades, home owners have seen consistent appreciation of their property value, leading to a steady rise of household wealth.

Notwithstanding its many benefits, public housing has emerged as a hot political issue. There is genuine concern that the rising cost of public housing has made it difficult for some to enter the housing market. Lum Sau Kim and Zhou Xuefeng's analysis in their paper "Is Housing Still Affordable?: New Disaggregated Indicators" shows a regressive pattern in housing affordability between 2000 and 2011 for the lower ranks of the income distribution, with the lowest income households facing the greatest degree of erosion in affordability.

High asset value is a desired public good, but it also means high entry cost in owning a home. It appears that a balance has to be found between the two and the government has taken action to reduce the entry cost of public housing. In his 2013 National Day Rally speech, the Prime Minister assured the working class population that no one will be priced out of public housing. It will be interesting to see if the reduction of the entry price and political assurance of affordability will settle this housing issue. But as Christopher has pointed out, the future asset value of the public housing may be negatively affected by the abundance of housing stock owned by the elderly population. The expected fall in asset value may become another hot issue for future policy debate.

3. CONCLUSION

Is life getting better in Singapore? Life is definitely good for the majority of the population. Singapore will continue to be ranked highly on any measure of national well-being on account of its solid economic growth, stable social environment, and strong urban services. However, the key social institutions established by the government since nationhood, is now being put to the test. Will the 3M health financing system, the public housing scheme, the CPF-based financial security arrangement, and the upward mobility guarantee, still be able to function as well as in the past? This volume will show that some serious issues exist and these long-standing schemes may require fine tuning to meet future needs.

CHAPTER 2

INCLUSIVE GROWTH

Growing Inclusivity, Addressing Labor Market Shortfalls and Enhancing International Competitiveness

SPEAKER: ASSOCIATE PROFESSOR TAN KHEE GIAP
Lee Kuan Yew School of Public Policy, National University of Singapore

1. INTRODUCTION

In his address to the Economic Society of Singapore (ESS) on 9 April 2012, Professor Lim Chong Yah proposed a series of shock therapies that could help close the widening income gap in Singapore and reduce its dependence on foreign workers.

His main proposal was for those earning below $1500 a month to get pay rises of 15% in the first year, a further 15% in the second year and 20% in the third year of the restructuring. Over the same period, his plan also called for a wage freeze for those earning above $15,000 a month. Those people falling in between would get an annual pay rise of around 4% to 5%.

The alternative suggested by Secretary-General Lim Swee Say of the National Trades Union Congress (NTUC) is to focus on upgrading and matching skills, and to redesign job contents; while the National Wages Council (NWC) has, since 1986, maintained that wage growth would have to lag behind productivity growth.

In defending this drastic second round of wage restructuring in Singapore, Prof. Lim also argued that the first high wage policy in restructuring the Singapore economy from 1979–1981 had been successful. Some analysts have pointed out the high wage policy has in fact contributed to the recession in 1985 by pushing wages beyond productivity and resulted in a serious loss of international competitiveness. ACI the financial markets association has done some empirical work and discovered that while increasing wage above productivity has indeed led to a loss in international competitiveness during the period, the strong exchange rate and the global downturn in the electronics cycle in 1984 as well as the regional slowdown have also contributed to the severity of the decline in 1985.

We share the same concern as Prof. Lim on the danger of widening income disparity, and for the plight of the low-income earners whose real wages have fallen due to the competitive pressure from the inflow of foreign workers. These we think are the core message Prof. Lim is trying to address. However, there are many ways to skin a cat as Prof. Lim himself acknowledged, when he noted that his wage-restructuring proposal is but one way of achieving inclusive growth.

2. ENHANCING INTERNATIONAL COMPETITIVENESS THROUGH WAGES–PRODUCTIVITY–COMPETITIVENESS (WPC) NEXUS

Singapore's highly open labor market, characterized by "one market, two remuneration" extremes, resulted from international competition both at the top tier and at the bottom tier with the middle being further parted in between the two. The consequences are rather obvious but challenging.

Ideally all Singaporeans would like to somehow move steadily and directly from Quadrant A (Fig. 1), exhibiting low wage, low productivity stalemate toward the high wage, high productivity of inclusive competitiveness, or Quadrant D.

The thrust of Prof. Lim's proposal amounts to moving from the current Quadrant A directly to the Quadrant B, which hopefully would reach Quadrant D. In contrast, the core of the NTUC–NWC hybrid described earlier amounts to moving from Quadrant A to Quadrant C (i.e., a low wage, high productivity hybrid) and eventually to arrive at Quadrant D.

The serious problem many European economies currently faced depicts a classic case of loss in competitiveness as in Quadrant B or the

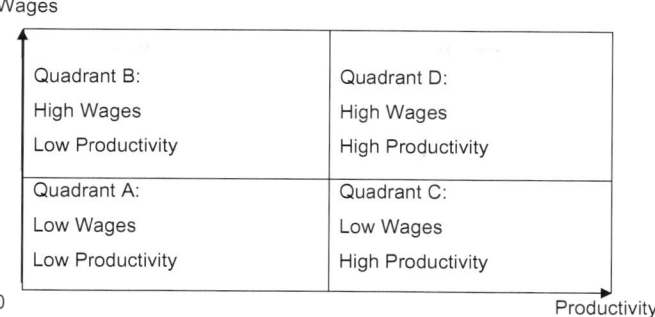

Figure 1. Wages–Productivity Nexus.

high wage, low productivity trap. In a competitive globalized world, this is not sustainable as wages are contained at lower levels, with union leaders who are focused largely on wage and not job maximization.

Quadrant A, or the low wage, low productivity stalemate that Singapore is experiencing, clearly is another classic case of labor market failure distorted by abundant supply of cheap foreign workforce in a number of industries with minimal incentive for employers to drive productivity.

Employees themselves are naturally reluctant or unable to put in their best performance given the poor effort–remuneration wage structure; productive local workforce tend to shun away from those industries because stagnated low wages are unmatched by the rising cost of living.

However, the NTUC–NWC's Quadrant C may not be sufficient either, as up-skill tends to take a longer time to materialize and current manpower policies on foreign workers, which are abundant in supply, tend to suppress wages at the local blue collar end unless co-ordinated further through government efforts.

3. THE FACILITATIVE ROLE OF THE GOVERNMENT TO CORRECT LABOR MARKET FAILURE

Hence, the Workfare Income Supplement (WIS) scheme came into being, though insufficient as it is with no direct linkage to productivity and a heavy state burden to say the least. Yet, WIS is much needed by Singaporeans in their late 40s and early 50s, who had limited opportunities for post-secondary education, and are currently facing skill mismatch and skill obsolescence exacerbated by rapid globalization.

It is thus paramount that the government must continue to proactively play the facilitative role of addressing labor market failure through the annual budgetary measures in the form of *targeted special transfers*, to avoid wasting of precious financial resources as exemplified in the 2012 Budget statements.

It is important to bear in mind that populist public policies, however well-intended, could have unintended consequences that could in turn cause market distortions that would be costly and take years to reverse. The government should resolutely resist the increasing pressure of being pushed toward the slippery road of becoming a welfare state, which is least sustainable in the longer-run, as we often argued, for a small and resource-poor economy such as Singapore.

The much-talked about non-market oriented non-productivity linked Minimum Wage Policy (MWP) is not practical either because once legislated, it cannot discriminate against non-Singaporeans. Foreign workers would have to be paid at the minimum wage acceptable for Singaporeans, even if they are prepared to accept a much lower wage.

The MWP in fact amounts to equating cost of living between Singapore and those cheaper neighboring countries, which would result in potential loss of government revenues from foreign workers' levies that can be gainfully deployed to improve the well-being of Singaporeans.

The paramount role of the government must be to ensure continuing economic restructuring, diligently monitor unit business costs, and most of all, to constantly ensure social mobility so as to safeguard against emergence of economic underclass or permanent underclass. We thus have the following six suggestions for consideration.

3.1. Rationalising Foreign Workforce to Correct Labor Market Structure, Improve Labor Market Efficiency and Overcome the Low Wage, Low Productivity Stalemate

For statutory declaration in application for Employment Passes, human resources managers ought to satisfy themselves in ensuring their requests are of "needed skill contents" that are unavailable locally and that solicitations amongst resident workforce were conducted with their sources of search declared. It is not realistic to expect the Ministry of Manpower (MOM) to justify "real needs" of employers in specific industries.

Industries or sub-sectors with jobs that are non-traded and of public service nature with government subsidies and serve to share cost burden such as public transportation, including bus and train operators, should have a "Singapore-First Policy" (SFP); where remuneration is set online with productivity to mitigate wage suppressing effect from cheap foreign workforce. For decades, the practice of such unannounced SFP has been and is still in operation for the taxi-driving profession, which could be expanded to other industries where Singapore's international competitiveness is not compromised.

Foreign workforce policies in co-ordination with SFP should be industry-specific, tailor-made with a ceiling quota, projected and announced three years ahead to facilitate business cost calculation and manpower planning.

Employers in the construction sector and, to some extent, in the hotel and restaurant industries, typically have little incentive to replace the widely available cheap supply of blue-collar foreign workforce in the region with mechanized equipment or processes, if it makes no difference to their bottom lines. Government effort, structured programs and time path will be needed to make the expected and necessary transition and changes.

On the other hand, as in the case of high-skill sectors such as life sciences, precision engineering and high-tech manufacturing activities, there should not be foreign workforce constraints where skilled labor shortages can only be filled in by foreigners. Similar argument could be made for cases of low-paying jobs, be it in the manufacturing or services sector, where local workforce is not forthcoming. Headcount ceilings should therefore be reviewed where labor productivity and production efficiency can be re-examined.

3.2. Proactive and Targeted Management in Skill Matching, Skill Upgrading, Job Skill Contents Re-Designing and Comprehensive Education Investment in Indigenous Manpower to Equip with Modern Skill-in-Demand

The MOM, with information on actual online job vacancies through requests for Employment Passes, S Passes, and Work Permits by employers, could actively co-ordinate with the Workforce Development Agency (WDA) to further improve employability for Singaporeans. WDA could make available a list of online resident job seekers gathered through various self-help groups, including the Chinese Development Assistance Council (CDAC); MENDAKI (Council for the Development of Singapore Malay/Muslim Community); Singapore Indian Development Association (SINDA); community development councils, and chambers of commerce, for comprehensive job placement and skill matching.

We further propose a younger cut-off age for qualification in the Reformed Workfare Income Supplement (RWIS) scheme, which could last for a maximum of three years, conditional upon participation in designated up-skill programmes sponsored by employers, where RWIS would pay for the market wage differential. Through up-skill and productivity enhancement, recipients would graduate from the RWIS scheme, once their skills are valued above government-defined Monthly Living Wage (MLW). Proper safeguards could be put in place to prevent abuse by unscrupulous employers.

It is paramount that all Singaporeans be equipped with future skills in demand from young; and the playing field in education be leveled, specifically for pre-school education, which should be made part of the national education commitment in the next decade. Going forward, the challenge is to invest in the younger generation of Singaporeans with comprehensive education and modern skill sets compatible with first-world living standards.

3.3. Changing the Fundamental Philosophy of Public Policies in Pursuit of Optimal, Inclusive, Balanced, Green and Clean Growth as a Small Open Economy

It is unwise for the government to curtail employment growth — thereby diluting robust economic growth during good times — because of public resistance to the presence of a large foreign workforce, or from other socialpolitical pressures. Such populist approaches could spell trouble for prudent governance; it is unrealistic to expect the government to regularly dip into its funds for special transfers or sustained balanced budgets for the full-term of the elected government, should the future be riddled by a higher frequency of recessions propelled by global conditions.

It is timely that we re-examine the fundamental philosophy of our public policies by re-defining the new role of the government, in pursuit of an even more inclusive society in our optimal growth strategies. It is important to reiterate that the government must continue to recognize market force as an essential benchmark for policy formulations and signposts for economic development in the pursuit for optimal, inclusive, balanced, green and clean (OIBGC) growth. However, exceptions should be considered when public services involve a hybrid of market benchmark and government subsidies, and the recent public funding of public transportations infrastructure in buses and trains are cases in point.

Computation of Unit Business Costs (UBC) consists of many cost components including wages, government charges, rentals, land costs, and others. Cost escalations driven by government charges, rentals, and land costs are considered by employers as a "*given*". They thus look for other avenues to mitigate UBC and often resort to wage containment, be it voluntary as part of the internal wage control or market-driven as part and parcel of the abundant supply of foreign workforce.

Hence, public policies that use market as benchmarks, while instilling discipline on government agencies for cost curtailment, efficiency, and minimization of deficit, can unintentionally lead to higher business costs, which in turn can severely lead to low wage and low productivity and aggravate income disparity.

3.4. Re-Defining Key Performance Indicators, Strengthening Policy Mechanisms and Financial Budget Allocations of Government Agencies

The Housing and Development Board (HDB) could consider revamping the affordability index for public housing pricing and rentals in order to appropriately reflect weights assigned according to room-types and income brackets. The National Environment Agency (NEA) could look at the cost-of-living index in relation to the government's defined MLW when setting the rental and base-price bidding for hawker stalls. The Public Transport Council (PTC) could re-examine the formula for setting public transportation fares by indexing it to affordability according to per capita household income, age groups, and inflation. Jurong Town Corporation (JTC) could review land costs, factory rentals and selling prices for Small and Medium Enterprises (SMEs), based on feasibility of business proposals to be judged by an independent committee led by the private sector.

Key performance indicators for various government agencies — apart from indicators such as cost curtailment, efficiency, and minimization of deficit, as disciplined by market-base benchmarks — may include surveys on customers' satisfaction, especially for industries where excessive foreign workers dominate, and where public services are involved and public interests are at stake. Revenue maximization and the minimization of subsidies would not be the necessary, nor sufficient condition when evaluating performances of government agencies. From the productivity view point, it is pertinent to take note or guard against Parkinson's Law, which argues that "work expands so as to fill the time available for its completion", a symptom prevailing in civil services worldwide.

These new inclusive approaches above would necessarily lead to lower revenues or bigger subsidies for statutory boards, ministries, and government-linked companies, but they would also translate into higher income and employment for Singaporeans. It is certainly superior to a more expensive, fiscally debilitating comprehensive social safety net proposed in some quarters.

3.5. Ensuring a Competitive Environment and a Level Playing Field for SMEs

It is pertinent to note that latest data available from the Department of Statistics (DOS) revealed that SMEs make up 99% of the 160,000 enterprises in Singapore, which employ 60% of the total workforce and contribute to more than 50% of her gross domestic product (GDP). It is thus an untapped potential, an important buffer for unemployment and a significant social stabilizer not to be overlooked, especially in times of external-driven shocks. Yet, years of brutal open competition and market forces have contributed to prolonged low productivity with undesirable outcomes.

To ensure thriving SMEs, we must monitor other components of UBC such as land cost, rental, fees, and charges. It is important to note that once these business costs are taken as a *"given"*, the squeeze would inevitably be on wage cost. As the manufacturing share of GDP would not doubt decline over time, the missions of JTC in allocating land and as factory landlord, must be revised accordingly to cater for SMEs in services as well, rather than limited to manufacturing activities as in the present case.

Comprehensive effort by government agencies are critical, such as nurturing Singapore's SMEs through improving their management via the Standards, Productivity and Innovation Board (SPRING Singapore); upgrading for professionals, managers, executives, and technicians (PMETs) through Human Capital Singapore (HCS); establishing better international network, marketing, and branding skills by International Enterprise (IE) Singapore; and renewing the effort by the Economic Development Board (EDB) as a link between multinational corporations (MNCs) and SMEs to invest in alternative locations such as Batam and Bintan. These initiatives would make a difference to employment creation for Singaporeans, improvement in wages and productivity for SMEs; if successful, it would mean a significant progress toward the objectives of the 2009 Economic Strategies Committee (ESC).

3.6. Persistence in Sharpening Singapore's International Competitive Edge, Plugging Further into the Globalization of Trade and Finance and Maintaining First-World Living Standards

Persistence in sharpening Singapore's international competitive edge and plugging into the globalization process are the only ways to maintaining Singapore's first-world living standards. Going forward, Singapore Inc. is going to be more and not less dependent on external demand, with highly differentiated and constantly renewed local and foreign talents.

Economic restructuring and productivity upgrading are an on-going process of self-renewal, and not just reactionary or one-off measures to tackle economic crises. We should have a continuous series of periodic Economic Review Committees (ERCs), even when the economy growth functions smoothly. There is no end date or "auto-piloting" for economic restructuring and productivity drive in an increasingly competitive globalized world.

We therefore propose to establish a high-level bi-annual national WPC taskforce consisting of members that represent diverse interest groups, with the following terms of references:

1. Evaluate the social profile and constraints of low wage Singaporeans and the emerging economic underclass.
2. Better understand industry-specific manpower issues, business difficulties, labor market requirements and expectations.
3. Explain and educate the public at large on the urgency of productivity drive, international labor market competition and improved work discipline.

4. COMMENTS ON PRESENTATION BY SPEAKER

Discussant: Mr Yeoh Lam Keong

Vice-President, Economic Society of Singapore

First, I completely agree with Associate Professor Tan Khee Giap's point that besides expanding social welfare and safety nets, we need to expand social support and services not just in areas where the government is traditionally strong, but also where we have allowed provision and access by the average citizen to slip behind real need. These are mainly in the areas of public housing, health care, and education. These are social service areas that are key to citizen welfare and where market failure is pronounced, there intelligent state provision makes a huge difference to median access. In public housing, the price of an entry-level three-room flat, say in Sengkang, is well over $300,000, making it five to six times the median household income. Just 10–15 years ago, such a flat would have sold for closer to two to three times the median income, as the HDB is also transferring the market price of residential land, which has been on an uptrend. This is unnecessary as we still have old land banks that were acquired much more cheaply and could be made available at book cost to the public. Existing property prices could be shielded from deflationary impacts by giving direct subsidies to first-time owners. Ideally, entry-level public housing for median families should be made available to the public at two to three times the median household income, as otherwise the repayment period would be too long and hamper adequate liquid savings by households. It has led to the perception that even basic public housing is becoming unaffordable and that the next generation would face significantly lower living standards.

In the area of health care, out-of-pocket expenditures are still generally too high, such that even middle-class families would have problems paying medical bills when they are elderly or encounter chronic illness. Universal health access is much better in other advanced Asian countries like South Korea, Taiwan, and Hong Kong, where the proportion of out-of-pocket health care expenses is much lower as they have higher levels of social safety nets compared to that in Singapore. Health care spending needs to rise from 1.5% of GDP currently to around 4%–5% of GDP over time, for adequate universal access without sacrificing quality. There has also been significant underinvestment in public health care facilities.

In education, the excessively competitive syllabus and low teacher–pupil ratio means that much of education has effectively been privatized in the tuition industry. Adding in the costs of tuition, education costs are high and escalating, worsening social mobility markedly. Again, we need to spend closer to the Organization for Economic Co-operation and Development (OECD) average of 6% of GDP on education rather than the current 3.7%; focus on adequate teacher–pupil ratios that would facilitate enough teaching for the average student; as well as reduce unnecessary competitive mass streaming. Finland, for example, has a teacher–pupil ratio of around 1:15 or 1:20, and could thus rely more on individual coaching and assessment. Their international scores for mathematics, science, and reading are as good as Singapore's.

Secondly, I also agree with the point that we should not have Scandinavian levels of social welfare spending, at close to 15%–20% of GDP. Nevertheless, I disagree that we should therefore not expand social security spending as this is a "slippery slope" that cannot withstand populist demand. Our social welfare and social security spending is relatively miniscule and we could well afford to increase this by 2%–3% of GDP. In particular, WIS needs to be doubled or trebled from $400 million to $1–1.5 billion per annum, to take care of the working poor at the bottom 10%–20% of the income scale. This would still only amount to around 0.5% of GDP. We also need some form of unemployment protection as well as support to retirement adequacy. A targeted means-tested pension grant is necessary to help around 300,000–400,000 older, less educated low-income workers who would otherwise have serious retirement adequacy problems. At the median level, the Central Provident Fund (CPF) interest rate should be raised significantly toward what was actually earned by Government of Singapore Investment Corporation (GIC), as this would make a big difference in retirement adequacy for the average citizen. Plenty of advanced democratic countries (Canada, Australia, Switzerland, New Zealand, and Hong Kong) are able to manage social security spending within fiscally sustainable limits.

Third, I completely disagree with the point made by Associate Professor Tan Khee Giap's analysis of long-term growth potential and targets, especially with respect to immigration and labor supply. Associate Professor Tan Kee Giap's and Adjunct Professor Tan Kong Yam's analysis suggest that we could have both higher labor supply growth and higher productivity growth. This is counter to our experience, where high labor supply growth has retarded productivity growth by making cheap labor preferable to investing in capital, skills or organization; as well as to the experience of other advanced countries, where both labor productivity and wages are significantly higher because of more restrictive immigration. In Hong Kong, for example, construction workers, plumbers, and nurses earn 1.5 to 3 times more than in Singapore for largely this reason. It is necessary to restrict labor supply through tight immigration over the next 10–20 years so that our lower wage occupations, that had been artificially depressed by two decades of excessive immigration, can catch up to levels in advanced countries with similar levels of per capita GDP. This is the only way of countering the tendency toward wage stagnation from the forces of globalization.

CHAPTER 3

EDUCATION AND SOCIAL MOBILITY

Education and Intergenerational Mobility*

SPEAKER: ASSOCIATE PROFESSOR IRENE NG
Department of Social Work, National University of Singapore

1. INTRODUCTION

Education is viewed as a source of social mobility. It provides the means to higher earnings. Compulsory and free education equalizes the opportunities toward higher earnings for students from different socioeconomic strata. However, what education achieves in theory does not always materialize in reality. Where rich and poor children go to different schools of different quality, education instead becomes a source of inequality. Several studies have shown the effects of education systems on intergenerational mobility, a dynamic form of inequality that looks at inequality as persisting from parents to children. The reinforcing effect of education systems on intergenerational mobility becomes pertinent in light of the current widening inequality in Singapore (as detailed in the other chapters in this collection) and theoretical findings that income inequality leads to intergenerational immobility (Solon, 2004; Ho, 2010).

This chapter first reviews the evidence from intergenerational mobility research and compares their findings against Singapore's education system.

---

*This article is a localised version of Ng, Irene (2013). Education and intergenerational mobility in Singapore. *Educational Review*, 1–15. The article is available at http://www.tandfonline.com/doi/abs/10.1080/0013/91.1.2013.780008#, VEnKAfmUecI.

Conclusions from the comparative analysis suggest a need for considering systemic reforms. The next section explains intergenerational mobility and compares mobility levels of different countries. Next, Singapore's education system is described, followed by an analysis of studies on the association between education systems and mobility. In this section, Finland's system is compared to Singapore's, and student outcomes in the Programme for International Students Assessment (PISA) analyzed. The last section draws learning points to take away from this review study.

2. INTERGENERATIONAL MOBILITY

Economists measure intergenerational mobility using the following reduced form of equation:

$$Y_i^{child} = \alpha + \beta Y_i^{parent} + \varepsilon_i^{child} \tag{1}$$

where Y_i is the logarithmic income of the individual and ε_i is an error term. The measure of intergenerational mobility is thus β, which shows the extent to which the child's income depends on the parents' income. β takes values between 0 to 1, where 0 indicates that the child's income does not depend on the parents' income at all and 1 indicates that the child's income depends only on the parents' income. Hence, β and mobility are inversely related: a high mobility is reflected by a low β.

β has been used as the baseline comparison of intergenerational mobility across time and countries. However, the data requirements for an accurate measure of β can be onerous, and different studies have yielded different results, depending on the data constraints. Nevertheless, with the accumulation of studies using various methods to address the data constraints, the general consensus is that among the Western industrialized countries, the United States (US) and the United Kingdom (UK) have the lowest mobility while Scandinavian countries have the highest mobility. The other European countries lie somewhere in between. A review by Black and Devereux (2010) suggests that $\hat{\beta}$ (the estimated value of β) is around 0.5 to 0.6 for the US, 0.3 for the UK and "almost always" lower than 0.3 for Scandinavian countries. The lowest mobility have been from less industrialized countries such as South Africa ($\hat{\beta}$ = 0.61; Hertz, 2001) and Brazil ($\hat{\beta}$ = 0.69; Dunn, 2007). There have also been studies on other developing countries [see Grawe (2004) on Ecuador, Nepal, Pakistan, Peru, and Malaysia]. However, the data on which these one-off studies are based are very limited, and mobility scholars have refrained from making conclusions on the correlation between development and mobility.

In Singapore, I published my first study on intergenerational mobility in 2007. Since then, I have published two more updates (Ng et al., 2009; Ng, 2012), and the Singapore Ministry of Finance (MOF) has published a report giving its own results and conclusions (Yip, 2012). Although my studies were based on a highly limited dataset, I applied the statistical methods used in the field to correct for the limitations. The limitations included a small sample size, a one-time and cross-sectional dataset; income reported in categories; income of parents reported by youth; income of youth reported at the beginning of their careers; and income of parents reported at the end of their careers. The statistical correction techniques that were applied include instrumenting long-term income with education and occupational status (across all three studies); replicating the data limitations on a US dataset (Ng et al., 2009); and scaling (Ng, 2007, 2012) to transform from earnings to income, and to reflect the peak earning age of 45 years in Corak (2006). The latest study pooled the samples in the National Youth Surveys 2002 and 2010 for a total sample size of 400 (Ng, 2012). It found a $\hat{\beta}$ of 0.24 before scaling and 0.44 after scaling. This was for young adults aged 23 to 29 in the respective survey years.

The MOF study had far superior data; its census, survey, and administrative data yielded a main sample size of 39,500 youths who were aged 30 to 39 in 2008. However, it did not correct for two key limitations, namely, that only five years of income data were used and the relatively older age of parents, in the study. Its $\hat{\beta}$ of 0.28 to 0.30 is therefore slightly underestimated.

While I concluded that mobility is moderately low, Yip concluded that mobility is moderate in Singapore. Combined, intergenerational mobility can be considered at most moderate for Singaporeans born between 1969 and 1979 (i.e., the birth years of sample offspring in National Youth Survey 2002 and the MOF study, excluding the 129 from the National Youth Survey 2010, who were born between 1981 and 1987). These cohorts had experienced only some of the changes in the education system that might have detrimental effects on intergenerational mobility.

28 Inequality in Singapore

3. SINGAPORE'S EDUCATION SYSTEM

In the years immediately after independence, the urgency for education resulted in a massive effort in building schools, the standardization of curriculum and the centralization of teacher training through the Ministry of Education (MOE) (Ng et al., 2009). However, as the need for basic education and literacy has been largely met, the education system had to contend next with new challenges. One of the main aims of Singapore's education system has been and continues to be producing a globally competitive workforce (Lee et al., 2008). In the early days, competitiveness of the labor force was met by quickly educating its residents. As Singapore's economy developed toward more high-technology and skills-intensive industries, the challenge becomes providing more differentiation in education such that the brightest are not held back by lower performers, and those lagging behind can learn at their own pace (Tan, 2010). Lee et al. (2008) described the educational focus as one that was "efficiency-driven" in the 1980s and 1990s, and "ability-driven" thereafter. Whether "efficiency-driven" or "ability-driven", the main role of education continues to be meeting economic needs, and the belief that different individuals are endowed with different abilities motivated an education system that emphasizes a tailored approach.

Figure 1 maps the timeline of various initiatives that increasingly differentiated the educational paths of students. In the first set of educational reforms, different forms of streaming according to academic ability were

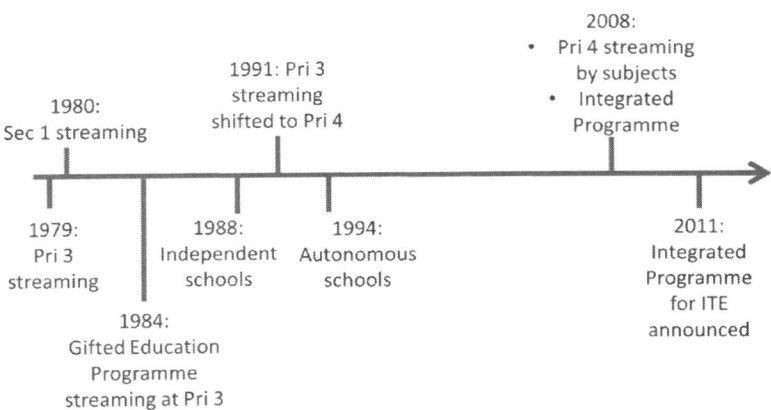

Figure 1. Milestones in the Decentralization of Singapore's Education System.

progressively rolled out. This began in 1979, when streaming was introduced at the end of Primary 3. In 1991, the streams were revamped and moved to Primary 4. In 2008, Primary 4 streaming was further revamped to "subject-based banding", which differentiates students by the number and types of subjects they study. This change was to allow students to take their best subjects at a higher level and weaker subjects at a more foundational level (Ministry of Education, 2011a, 2011b).

Streaming for secondary school was introduced in 1980. This occurs through the Primary School Leaving Examination (PSLE) at the end of Primary 6. Depending on their results, students are currently streamed into three possible tracks: normal technical, normal academic, and express. The different streams in secondary school are geared toward different post-secondary institutions. The two normal streams lead to the 'N' Level examination, taken at the end of Secondary 4. The 'N' Level qualifies students for the Institute of Technical Education (ITE). Normal academic students with better 'N' Level results can also go on to Secondary 5 to take the 'O' Level examination, which Express stream students take at Secondary 4. The 'O' Level examination sorts students into polytechnics or junior colleges, to prepare for universities. After two years of junior college education, students take the 'A' Level examination, which qualifies them for local universities.

Although there are three broad streams, there is further differentiation within the streams. In the Express stream, the Integrated Programme (IP) was introduced in 2008 (Ministry of Education, 2011a, 2011b). The IP allows students to by-pass the 'O' Level examination and "optimize the time freed up from preparing for the 'O' Level examination to stretch the brighter students and provide greater breadth in the academic and non-academic curriculum" (Ministry of Education, n. d.). IP students therefore go straight to the 'A' Level, or in some schools, take the International Baccalaureate (IB) examination instead. At the other end, a through track for the best students in the Normal tracks has also been created to enable entry into ITE and later polytechnic without having to sit for the 'O' Level examination (Ministry of Education, 2010).

In addition to streaming and the integrated programs, some students are also selected into the Gifted Education Programme (GEP). This was introduced in 1984 through a test at Primary 3. Students who were not "discovered" and did not join the GEP at Primary 3 could be selected into the GEP when entering Secondary 1. At secondary school, the GEP is blended into the IP.

In addition, the different streams and programs are offered by different schools, and schools have been increasingly decentralized. In 1988, the first independent schools were approved; they were allowed to set their own curriculum, hire their own teachers and charge their own fees. There are currently eight independent schools listed in Singapore (Ministry of Education, 2012b), all of which offer GEP, and seven of which offer IP. IP is also offered by four other schools, and was to be expanded to seven more schools from 2010 onwards. Most of the independent schools offer only IP, and neither the independent schools nor the schools with IP offer the normal streams of secondary education (Ministry of Education, 2012a, 2011b).

After rolling out independent schools in 1988, autonomous schools were introduced in 1994. Although autonomous schools that still report to the central Education Ministry, received higher funding for greater pedagogical freedom, charged more affordable fees than the independent schools did (Tan, 2010). Other area-specific specialized schools such as the Sports School and School of the Arts have also been introduced, and specialized schools for normal technical education are expected to commence operations in 2013 (Ministry of Education, 2010).

It is evident then that Singapore's education system places emphasis on developing, early on, different types of students in different environments. Secondary schools can be ranked according to their average entry, PSLE scores and their exit 'O' Level or 'A' Level scores, with the independent schools at the top, autonomous schools in the mid-range, and what has now been termed "neighbourhood schools" at the bottom. In terms of preparation for higher education, therefore, IP students are geared not only toward local universities, but also toward top universities overseas. At the other end of the academic continuum, normal technical stream students are geared toward studies in the vocational institutions of ITE.

Tertiary education in Singapore is highly subsidized for citizens. According to the Government Budget 2010, the subsidy rates were up to 75% for university and 85% for polytechnics. These subsidy rates have decreased from the past. Further, since corporatization of the two state universities in 2006 and the introduction of other state-supported universities, tuition fees have also been gradually raised. Nevertheless, university tuition fees continue to be low compared to countries such as the UK and the US. Many bursaries for poorer students are also available.

Vocational education was established as post-secondary training in 1992 with the establishment of ITE. This replaced the Vocational and Industrial Training Board (VITB), which students typically joined after Secondary 2. The overhaul was deemed necessary, as vocational education was viewed negatively; it "became 'dumping grounds' or 'catch-nets' for those who failed to measure up to the requisite academic rigor" (Lee *et al.*, 2008). Since then, the ITE has greatly expanded its programs, with advance certifications and pathways to polytechnic education. ITE campuses have been transformed into state-of-the art facilities. ITE has now become world-renowned and award-winning. However, the low image of an ITE certification might not have improved much, especially in light of the widening wage gap between professional and technical jobs.

4. EFFECT OF EDUCATION SYSTEM ON INTERGENERATIONAL MOBILITY

It is clear that the Singapore education system has introduced many different tracks for students, beginning at a young age of nine and continuing on throughout secondary school, until they are sorted into different post-secondary institutions. The rationale is to create many pathways to success. Unfortunately for intergenerational immobility, the current evidence suggests that the changes in Singapore's education system have reinforcing effects on immobility, which this section discusses in three parts, in relation to: (a) uniformity of the education system; (b) expansion and corporatization of tertiary education; and (c) progressivity in public expenditure on education.

4.1. Uniformity

The increasing differentiation — through school-based streaming and types of schools with different fees and curricula — looks to have segregating effects that are detrimental to mobility. Theoretical models have found that more homogeneous systems (i.e., public rather than private systems) beget greater intergenerational mobility (Davies *et al.*, 2005; Ho, 2010). In empirical research, a most compelling study by Pekkarinen *et al.* (2009) had the advantage of a natural experiment from a comprehensive school reform in Finland during the years 1972 to 1975. It exploited the fact that changes happened at different times in different school districts. The reform shifted the streaming to academic and vocational tracks from ages 11 to 16, replacing the two-track system in Singapore's equivalent of primary and secondary education with a uniform nine-year system. There are also no high-stakes national examinations in Finland. These changes, which made the education system more uniform, were found to decrease intergenerational income correlation by 23% from 0.3 to 0.23.

While mobility enhancing, how does Finland's uniform education system measure up in terms of producing high-calibre students for a competitive workforce? This is a natural question beyond the assumption that equity comes at the price of performance. Two world rankings suggest that the performance of Finnish students is far from mediocre. First, in the Global Competitiveness Index (GCI) by the World Economic Forum (WEF), Finland was ranked fourth in 2011/2012, an improvement from seventh position in 2010/2011 and close to Singapore's second place. A key reason highlighted for Finland's ranking was its top rank in terms of higher education and training, which was attributed to "a strong focus on education over recent decades" which had "provided the workforce with the skills needed to adapt rapidly to a changing environment and has laid the groundwork for high levels of technological adoption and innovation" (World Economic Forum, 2012).

Second, Finnish students have been among the top performers in international students tests. In the PISA 2009 conducted by the Organization for Economic Co-operation and Development (OECD) on 15 year-olds, Finnish students excelled in all three subjects tested, outperforming Singaporean students in reading and science, and losing to Singaporean students only in mathematics (Table 1).

Further, within-country variation in PISA scores reveals Finland to be superior in terms of parity between students. In several measures of parity, Finland tends to be amongst the most equitable. Singapore, on the other hand, tends to fall within the "inequitable" half of the spectrum, although

Table 1. PISA Scores of Top 12 Ranked Economies (2009).

Rank	Reading (Overall)		Mathematics		Science	
	Economy	Score	Economy	Score	Economy	Score
1	China: Shanghai	556	China: Shanghai	600	China: Shanghai	575
2	Korea	539	Singapore	562	Finland	554
3	Finland	536	Hong Kong	555	Hong Kong	549
4	Hong Kong	533	Korea	546	Singapore	542
5	Singapore	526	Chinese Taipei	543	Japan	539
6	Canada	524	Finland	541	Korea	538
7	New Zealand	521	Liechtenstein	536	New Zealand	532
8	Japan	520	Switzerland	534	Canada	529
9	Australia	515	Japan	529	Estonia	528
10	Netherlands	508	Canada	527	Australia	527
11	Belgium	506	Netherlands	526	Netherlands	522
12	Norway	503	China: Macao	525	Chinese Taipei	520
	OECD Average	493	OECD Average	496	OECD Average	501

it is not among the most unequally distributed (OECD, 2010). For illustrative purposes, the next few paragraphs compare different measures of parity of the top 12 countries in mean reading score.

First, Fig. 2 shows the performance of the top 12 countries in reading. The vertical axis gives the mean reading scores while the horizontal axis gives the difference in reading scores between the 90th and 10th deciles. Finland's mean score ranks third, ahead of Singapore which ranks fifth. In addition, using the red dotted line to divide the 12 countries into countries with scores that are more unequal than the OECD average on the right and countries with more equal scores than the OECD average on the left, the top four scoring countries are on the left. The spread in Singapore's scores is less equal than the OECD average, although there are other countries in the top 12 that have more uneven scores.

A second type of measure that PISA has developed is the relationship between the PISA performance and an index of socioeconomic status (SES). Figure 3 shows two related measures of this relationship. On the horizontal axis is the "slope of the socioeconomic gradient", which

34 *Inequality in Singapore*

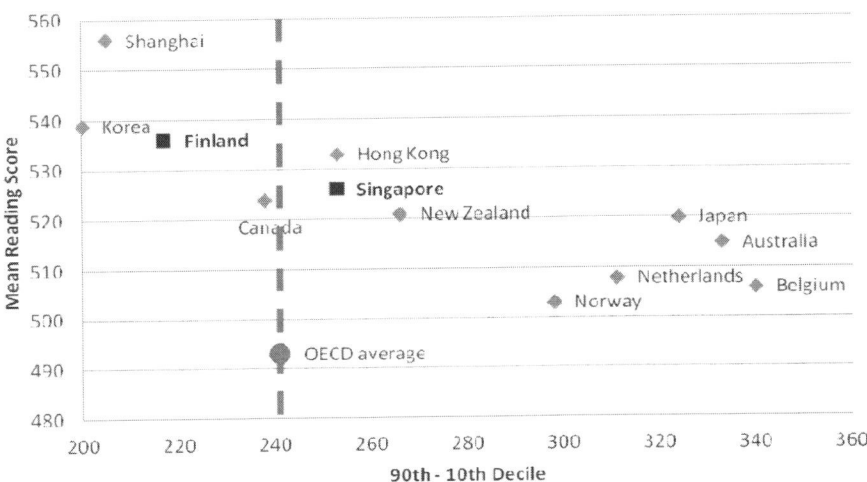

Figure 2. Mean Value and Distribution of PISA Reading Scores of Top 12 Economies.

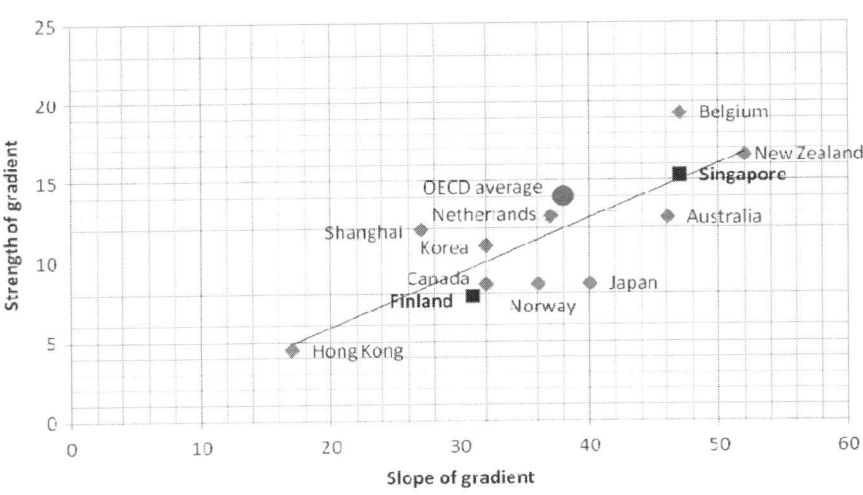

Figure 3. Relationship Between Reading Performance and Socioeconomic Background.

measures how much PISA scores improve with a unit change in the SES. Hence, in countries where there is a wide difference between students' scores that is also related to their socioeconomic background, the slope will be higher. On the vertical axis is the "percentage of variation in student performance explained by students' socioeconomic background." This measures the "strength" of the relationship between PISA performance and SES. Hence, the higher this number, the more SES determines PISA performance. According to OECD,

> "where the slope of the gradient is steep and the gradient is strong, the challenges are the greatest because this combination implies that students and schools are unlikely to 'escape' the close relationship between socioeconomic background and learning outcomes" (OECD, 2010).

Figure 3 shows that a linear line can be fitted to the scatter positions of the 12 economies, so that economies that have steep gradients also tend to be countries that have strong gradients. Among the 12 countries, Finland has the second lowest dependence of reading scores on SES, after Hong Kong. Singapore, on the other hand, has the third highest dependence of reading performance on SES, after Belgium and New Zealand. In a study by Hindriks *et al.* (2010), the reason for Belgium's high dependence of student performance on SES was attributed to streaming. In Belgium, students are streamed at 12 years old into three tracks: general, technical-arts, and vocational. Based on PISA 2006, the study concluded that school-based tracking was a main driver of the high correlation between SES and student PISA performance, which it referred to as "inequality of opportunity". It further explained that ability-based tracking resulted in inequality of opportunity through "the uneven distribution of social groups across schools", which it referred to as "social segregation" (Hindriks *et al.*, 2010).

Findings, such as this study in Belgium have important implications for Singapore, where streaming is also ability- and school-based. Getting into the best schools, GEP and IP have become so competitive that many parents who have the means, move to or rent addresses near elite schools, volunteer in their primary school of choice, and invest heavily in private tuition to prepare their children not only for the PSLE, but also for entry to GEP and IP (Toh, 2012; Chow, 2012). These are examples of advantages that well-resourced parents have over poorer parents that are facilitated by policies that give priority to school entry by proximity and existing ties that parents have to schools.

Contrary to the above patterns of results where Singapore rates more unequal than its contemporaries, however, Singapore (as well as most of

Table 2. Proportion of Resilient Students Among Top 12 Countries in Reading Score.

	Economy	% of resilient students
1	Shanghai	19
2	Hong Kong	18
3	Korea	14
4	Singapore	12
5	Finland	11
6	New Zealand	11
7	Japan	11
8	Canada	10
9	Australia	8
10	Netherlands	8
11	Belgium	8
12	Norway	6
	OECD average	8

the top 12 economies) have a higher percentage of resilient students than the OECD average. This result was also reported in *The Straits Times* (Davie, 2011). Among the top 12 economies, Singapore ranks fourth and Finland ranks fifth in the proportion of resilient students (Table 2). However, a closer look reveals that the definition of resilience itself results in economies where more students score high (and therefore have a high mean value) will have higher percentages of resilient students. Broadly, PISA considers a student resilient when his or her performance exceeds "the performance predicted by the average relationship among students from similar socioeconomic backgrounds across countries" (OECD, 2010). Since the benchmarks is the average of all OECD economies, economies with more students performing above the OECD average will tend to have higher percentage of resilient students.

Summarising the insights from PISA, two main learning points can be derived. First, while on average Singapore students outperform many students around the world, there appears to be less equity in learning opportunities and outcomes in Singapore than the international average.

Second, the example of Finland suggests that greater equity can be achieved without compromising standards. Finland's superior performance in both student scores and equity has been attributed to its comprehensive educational system (as opposed to systems with a public and private mix); emphasis on high teaching quality; and strong support for students (Sirkku *et al.*, 2009). The greater equity in Finland's education system is also consistent with the mobility enhancing effect found by Pekkarinen *et al.* (2009). While Sirkku *et al.* (2009) warned against "making (too) far-reaching conclusions for national education policies based on just one type of study", the PISA findings nevertheless provide important reflections of Singapore's system compared to one such as Finland's.

4.2. Tertiary Education

The second characteristic in Singapore's education scene, which the research suggests has detrimental effects on mobility is the expansion, privatization and increasing fees of tertiary education. Lefranc and Trannoy (2006) suggested that lower mobility in the US compared with Europe might be due to more expensive tertiary education in the US. Along the same vein, Blanden and Machin (2004) found that the expansion of university places in the UK had increased participation among high-income students more than among low-income students. Both studies show that access to tertiary education and in turn, access to an earning premium from a university degree is biased in favor of wealthier families. Therefore, expanding tertiary education might disadvantage poor students instead.

4.3. Government Spending

The third educational feature found to affect intergenerational mobility is public expenditure, where higher and more progressive spending on education (i.e., more spending on low-income students) yields greater intergenerational mobility (Ichino *et al.*, 2010; Solon, 2004). In Singapore, government investments in the education sector are large. After defence, education is the next largest area of government expenditure. In 2010, education comprised 26% of the government's operating expenditure and 31% of its development expenditure (Department of Statistics, 2011). All schools in Singapore

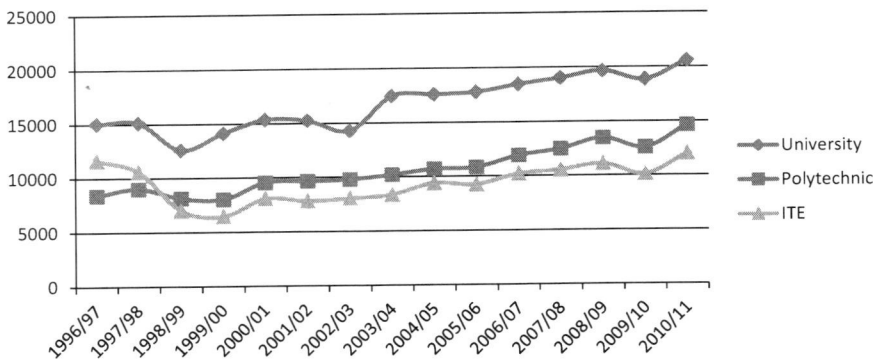

Figure 4. Government Post-Secondary Recurrent Expenditure Per Student.
Source: Ministry of Education (2011b).

are equipped with high-quality infrastructure and teachers. In the words of the current Minister of Education Heng Swee Keat, the MOE aims to ensure that "every school is a good school" (Wong, 2012). However, while it is necessary to ensure good baseline access and quality, a more pertinent consideration in terms of how education affects mobility, is whether the government spends more on wealthier students. Given that the elite schools have more students from wealthy backgrounds (Chang, 2011), it would be instructive to have data on government spending by type of school.

At the post-secondary level, Fig. 4 suggests that government spending is regressive. Except in 1996/1997 and 1997/1998, when government recurrent expenditure per student is higher in ITE than in polytechnics, the trend has been one of highest spending on university and lowest on ITE. Assuming that more students from rich families enter university and more students from poor families go to ITE, this translates into higher spending on richer students than poorer students. Furthermore, university students are in school for more years, and therefore benefit from government subsidies for a longer time.

The above conclusion is obviously an oversimplification, because overall expenditure covers different types of expenses, and not all of which are directly related to students' learning. For example, a large portion of university expenditure goes into research, although it can also be argued that it is usually university students that benefit from the rich research.

Further, given Singapore's educational ethos of developing talent and ability, regressive or non-progressive government expenditure is hardly unexpected. While there are bursaries for low-income students at various points in the education system, bursaries tend to be for a minority few, and cannot serve to counteract the immobility reinforcing characteristics of the main system. Bursaries are also means-tested, so that only applicants from the lowest income families qualify for them.

4.4. Effects of Education System on Intergenerational Mobility

Singapore's educational landscape contains at least two of the three characteristics above that generate intergenerational immobility. The overall system has decentralized and differentiated rapidly into an array of tracks that differentiate students by stream, program, subject type, and school. With such a system that research suggests will result in richer students attaining higher levels of qualification, the expansion of university places and decrease in tuition fees subsidy also serve to reinforce income advantages intergenerationally. The third characteristic on government expenditure requires more detailed data to ascertain whether its effects are likely mobility enhancing or curtailing. Overall, the lessons from overseas research suggest that there are characteristics of Singapore's education that need to be reconsidered in order to address concerns about intergenerational mobility. While the current intergenerational mobility found by Yip (2012), myself and my co-authors is not low, the cohorts that we studied have experienced the decentralization initiatives only partially. If the associations between educational policy and intergenerational mobility found in overseas literature are true, then mobility will become increasingly challenged.

5. CONCLUSIONS AND DISCUSSION

Below is a summary of the key findings and implications of this review study:

1. Intergenerational mobility is at most moderate in Singapore, but will be increasingly challenging given Singapore's education system, which has several characteristics that tend to reinforce intergenerational immobility. These characteristics include ability-based and

school-based streaming, privatization of basic and tertiary education, expansion of tertiary education while reducing subsidies, and possibly regressive public expenditure on education.
2. Given that Singapore's income inequality is one of the widest among developed economies and that income inequality leads to intergenerational immobility, addressing income inequality and intergenerational immobility need to take priority in national policy.
3. Government policies can and do shape intergenerational mobility. Thus, we do not have to accept immobility as an inevitable consequence of economic development.
4. A performance–equity trade-off, and in extension, a progress–mobility trade-off, might not necessarily be true. Thus, making intergenerational mobility a priority does not necessarily compromise on economic competitiveness.
5. Remedial and peripheral interventions have limited effectiveness in leveling up children from poorer backgrounds, if the overall system reinforces immobility. Thus, while interventions such as bursaries and early education intervention are important, systemic changes are necessary to prevent intergenerational immobility at the national level. Expanding remedial programs, standardizing early education or regulating private tuition can only do so much if entry into the main education system and the outcomes of students thereafter have social segregation effects that lead to unequal opportunities.

I have framed the conclusions in tentative terms, because they are based on current trends in Singapore and findings from overseas, not on actual evaluations of systems and programs in Singapore. There are limits to drawing lessons from comparing Singapore's system against overseas findings because there could be nuanced elements in Singapore's systems that are absent in the systems discussed in current research; elements that might mitigate the surface ill-effects on mobility. For example, although Singapore's public expenditure on education is likely regressive, that each track receives heavy monetary investments from the government might have mobility inducing effects not found in differentiated education systems elsewhere. Another example is that although tertiary education is being expanded and government subsidies reduced, tuition fees in

Singapore are low compared to those in the US and the UK, and bursaries might be more available and effective than in other countries.

All these require specific evaluations on the various characteristics to draw any conclusive evidence, tasks that are extremely data- and time-intensive. However, these evaluations are worthwhile in enabling our understanding of whether and how our systems affect intergenerational mobility. However, rigorous evaluations might take a long time, while the challenges of inequality and immobility are of increasing urgency.

With or without rigorous evaluations, overseas evidence on how systems affect mobility compels our honest reassessment of long-held beliefs of Singapore's education system; rethinking of the motivations of current policies; and rebalancing of priorities. For example, Singapore's education system emphasizes "equal opportunity for all." While few would argue that the current system does not provide opportunities, the real question in intergenerational mobility is: are opportunities truly equal? Further, are the "many pathways" to success too many? Will reducing the differentiation of the current system really compromise the competitiveness and talent development of students? Even if there is some compromise, what are the costs of keeping such a system in terms of the social segregation and mobility effects? To what extent should public funds be spent on grooming the brightest, and public policies help to create such selectivity, if they also serve to reproduce class advantage?

In practical terms, these questions call for a rethink of initiatives such as streaming and the increasing number of specialized schools; primary one admission through school location, parents' volunteering and pre-existing connections; and a national high-stakes examination at the early age of 12 that is tied to streaming and allocation to secondary schools. While recognising the limited role that public policies can play in regulating parents' private investments, educational policies also do not have to be the inductor of such private investments. The expansion of tertiary education should also proceed with greater attention to ameliorating the potential inequality effects. Borrowing the words of Education Minister Heng Swee Keat at his National Day Rally speech 2012, these "recalibrations" and "refreshing" of the education system would profoundly shape the futures of our children in the next 20 years and beyond.

6. COMMENTS ON PRESENTATION BY SPEAKER

Discussant: Associate Professor Tan Ern Ser

Department of Sociology, and Academic Convenor, Singapore Studies, Faculty of Arts and Social Sciences, National University of Singapore

6.1. Backdrop to the Debate

In the build-up to the 2011 General Election, an issue which assumed much prominence in the media is that of social mobility. This is hardly surprising, given that Singapore prides itself on being a land of opportunity, understood as one in which class origin does not significantly determine one's career and life trajectory. Indeed, in several visible ways-educational, occupational, and income attainment, home and car ownership, and standard of living — a majority of Singaporeans have experienced some degree of upward social mobility, some more so than others, most spectacularly in the 70s and early 80s. This has provided a concrete basis for the emergence of the Singapore version of the American dream.

Unfortunately, from the mid-80s onward, the Singapore dream has increasingly come under serious threat in the forms of economic fluctuations, global competition, cost inflation, and an ageing population, which lead to income inequality, employment and income insecurity, higher cost of living, and higher age-related support ratios. While these obstacles in the path of social mobility have, for better or for worse, not quite transformed the Singapore dream into a nightmare, they have produced some measure of anxiety, disillusionment, and frustration among Singaporeans. Apart from the sense of insecurity, even a fear of downward mobility, there is a concern that the widening income gap, and in turn the hardening of class boundaries, would act as a dampener on upward social mobility for those on the lower and middle segments of the social ladder, resulting in class origin largely determining destiny once again.

The above scenario constitutes the impetus for and backdrop to the recent and still current debate on social mobility in Singapore. At the risk of oversimplification, the debate can be construed as one between those who insist that social mobility is possible in Singapore, and those who argue that social mobility is less probable as we move down the social ladder.

6.2. The Debate

This debate was kindled by Irene Ng just before the election season. She fired the first salvo in a newspaper article with the catchy title "Growing worry of social immobility" (Ng, 2011b). In her article, she began by citing then Minister Mentor Lee Kuan Yew's observation that class, rather than merit, has a large part to play in primary school admissions, and university-educated parents are more likely to have children who qualify for the top secondary schools in Singapore. She then argued that the education playing field is uneven in which parents who possess the social capital to facilitate their children's entry into top primary schools, as well as the economic capital to invest in enhancing the human and cultural capital of their offspring, could ensure a better outcome for their next generation. She highlighted that her own empirical analysis, based on the National Youth Survey conducted in 2002 and 2005, indicates that Singapore's intergenerational mobility has been "moderately low compared with other developed countries".

Ng's article was promptly met with a response from the MOE that "social immobility is not a problem" here in Singapore (Cheong, 2011). In the rejoinder, Cheong Wei Yang, MOE's spokesperson, pointed out that pupils from neighborhood schools have consistently been represented among the top 5% of PSLE students. He also noted that almost half of the students from the lower housing types, i.e., one to three-room HDB flats — make it to tertiary-level institutions, which include both polytechnics and universities in the Singapore context. However, Cheong did not specify the extent to which students from the lower classes are represented among the top students in each cohort. Such data would provide some indication in regard to whether or not class origin matters as a determinant of social mobility.

In sociological parlance, Cheong has essentially highlighted the persistence of absolute social mobility in Singapore, while Ng's contention is that relative mobility rates decline as we move from the top of the social ladder to the bottom. Moreover, he took the opportunity to reiterate that meritocracy, which is one of Singapore's core values, has been consistently upheld by the education system. He concluded his rejoinder by affirming the government's policy of ensuring that "students are not denied opportunities to progress due to their financial circumstances", which translates into a more level playing field, and by implication, the insignificance of class and thereby the importance of merit in determining mobility chances.

Following the MOE's rejoinder, the then Minister for Education, Ng Eng Hen, gave a fairly detailed response during the parliamentary budget debate on his ministry on 7 March 2011. Given the chronological sequence, Minister Ng's speech came across as an elaboration of Cheong's rejoinder. Among other things, he provided several charts to prove his point that there is social mobility, even for those from lower SES. One of which compares the educational qualifications of two cohorts of Singaporeans aged 25 to 39, demonstrating the significant improvement in educational attainment in just one generation between 1980 and 2010. Another two charts present the educational performance of students from low socioeconomic backgrounds, showing the proportion who achieved high scores in the PSLE and the proportion who qualified for tertiary institutions. Minister Ng also provided details on the enormous resources continually pumped into the education system which have brought about a process analogized as a massive rising tide lifting every Singaporean along with it, subtly hinting that more than just pursuing the Singapore dream, Singaporeans have lived the Singapore story of upward social mobility for all. To underscore his argument that low SES is not a barrier to success, he highlighted the case of a pair of twins who did exceptionally well in their 'A' levels, despite their coming from a disadvantaged, low-income background.

Undoubtedly, there is a strong empirical basis to Minister Ng's argument that most Singaporeans have experienced some degree of upward social mobility over the last several decades. What is conspicuously absent in his message, however, are cross-class comparisons of mobility outcomes. He did provide a case study to demonstrate that low class origin is no hindrance to social mobility, even longer range ones. He also pointed out correctly that mobility outcomes need not be equal, given that ability, motivation, and efforts, including parental efforts, are likely to be unequal. But such an approach does not provide a convincing argument that relative mobility chances may turn out to be statistically similar across classes, that class advantages do not matter much in shaping career trajectories, or that significant mobility is highly probable, and not merely possible (Ng, 2011a).

Fortunately, the debate did not end at that point. In the months following the 2011 General Election, there has been a clear shift in the official orientation toward the issue of social mobility. Where Minister Ng focused on the massive rising tide of upward social mobility several months earlier, Prime Minister Lee Hsien Loong made the observation that Singapore society is "stratifying" and that "while the children of successful people are doing better, the children of less successful people are doing less well" (quoted in Cai and Heng, 2011). In the same news article, I added that social connections relating to class background matter, even in a meritocracy, and that "mobility chances are not the same across classes, despite policies aimed at equalizing opportunities".

With the re-orientation in thinking about social mobility in Singapore, the debate then shifted to determining the extent of class reproduction. In early January 2012, Yip Chun Seng, an economist at the MOF, released a paper, based on official data from a combination of administrative, survey, and census records, examining the income and education correlations between father–son pairs. This paper has in a sense brought the debate one full circle in that its objective, like that of the MOE rejoinder, is another rebuttal of Irene Ng's position on social mobility in Singapore. There is no doubt that Yip had the advantage of having access to a more robust dataset, as reflected in his using precise administrative data on income of 39,500 father–son pairs, compared to Irene Ng's meagre 271 parent-child pairs and their self-reported and therefore, less reliable income range figures. From his analysis, a large part of which involves making adjustments to reduce data bias and measurement errors, Yip concluded that the extent of mobility in Singapore for the cohorts he studied was "relatively high", compared to Irene Ng's less upbeat "moderately low" assessment. However, quite apart from the correlations, Yip also has one table showing that the proportion of children attaining university qualification is 0.72, given a father with university education; whereas the comparative figure for children from households in which the father has primary education is 0.20. Such figures indicate that while mobility is present across classes, the probability of getting to the higher rungs of the social ladder decreases as we move down the ladder, which is precisely Irene Ng's point in the first place.

6.3. Concluding Remarks

Having reviewed the chronology of arguments and counterarguments in the debate, one may make the following observations, which I believe would resonate with that of Irene Ng:

1. There is social mobility in Singapore.
2. Class origin does to some extent, even significantly, determine class destiny.
3. Mobility chances decline, moving down the social ladder. Logically speaking, it is possible for social immobility on some rungs of the social ladder to co-exist with social mobility occurring on other rungs of the ladder, thereby widening class inequality.
4. "Rags to riches" mobility is possible, but not highly probable.

Irene Ng's paper and subsequent presentation at the Institute of Policy Studies (IPS) also betray the need to have access to robust data. The comparison with Yip's paper points to the importance of having administrative data which government ministries possess in abundance; in the absence of which, academics can only rely on proxy data when far more precised ones are available. Perhaps, it's about time we explore how academics could, within the constraint of data privacy, collaborate with government ministries, using administrative data, to work on policy issues.

In her presentation, Irene Ng has suggested the critical role of education model in facilitating or hindering social mobility. She seems to favor the Finnish model, characterized by basic uniform education for students from ages 7 to 16 years; and the absence of high-stakes national examinations. While her presentation did not provide any definitive answers, it implies that there are good reasons to examine a broad range of education models and consider their impact on social mobility. This would move the debate on social mobility forward, and hopefully strengthen Singapore's ambition to be a land of equal opportunity where merit, rather than class, solely determines mobility outcomes, which, by definition, will understandably be unequal.

REFERENCES

Black, SE and PJ Devereux (2010). Recent developments in intergenerational mobility. Working paper No. 15889, National Bureau of Economic Research, Cambridge. http://www.nber.org/papers/w15889. Available at https:global.factive.com.

Blanden, J and S Machin (2004). Educational inequality and the expansion of UK higher education. *Scottish Journal of Political Economy*, 51(2), 230–249.

Cai, H and J Heng (2011). A chance to move up in life. *The Straits Times*, 29 October.

Chang, R (2011). Parents' background the edge for students at top schools: MM. *The Straits Times*, 25 January.

Cheong, WY (2011). Singapore's meritocratic education system promotes social mobility. *The Straits Times*, 23 February.

Chow, J (2012). Schools free to decide how parents volunteer. *The Straits Times*, 12 May.

Corak, M (2006). Do poor children become poor adults? Lessons from a cross country comparison of generational earnings mobility. *Research on Economic Inequality*, 13(1), 143–188.

Davie, S (2011). Poor students can score just as well. *The Straits Times*, 5 October.

Davies, JB, J Zhang and J Zeng (2005). Intergenerational mobility under private vs. public education. *Scandinavian Journal of Economics*, 107(3), 399–417. doi: 10.1111/j.1467-9442.2005.00415.x.

Department of Statistics, Singapore (2011). *Yearbase of Statistics 2010*.

Dunn, C (2007). The intergenerational transmission of lifetime earnings: Evidence from Brazil. *Berkeley Electronic Journal of Economic Analysis and Policy*, 7(2), 1–40.

Grawe, ND (2004). Intergenerational mobility for whom? The experience of high- and low-earning sons in international perspective. In *Generational Income Mobility in North America and Europe*, M Corak (ed.), pp. 58–89. Cambridge: Cambridge University Press.

Hertz, TN (2001). Education, inequality and economic mobility in South Africa. PhD dissertation, Amherst University of Massachusetts, Amherst.

Hindriks, J, M Verschelde, G Rayp and K Schoors (2010). Ability tracking, social segregation and educational opportunity: Evidence from Belgium. http://www.pcb.ub.edu/xreap/workshop/downloads/papers/avalunts/finals/hindriks-verschelde-rayp-schools.pdf.

Ho, KW (2010). Social mobility in Singapore. In *Management of Success: Singapore Revisited*, T Chong (ed.), pp. 217–241. Singapore: Institute of Southeast Asian Studies.

Ichino, A, L Karabarbounis and E Moretti (2010). The political economy of intergenerational income mobility. NBER working paper series no. 15946, National Bureau of Economic Research, Cambridge.

Lee, SK, CB Goh, B Fredriksen and JP Tan (eds.) (2008). *Toward a Better Future: Education and Training for Economic Development in Singapore since 1965*. Singapore: World Bank & National Institute of Education, Singapore.

Lefranc, A and A Trannoy (2006). Intergenerational earnings mobility: An evaluation using data on three generations. *Paper presented at the EALE 2006 Conference,* Prague: Charles University.

Ministry of Education, Singapore (n. d.). Education in Singapore. http://www.moe.edu.sg/about.

Ministry of Education, Singapore (2007). Many pathways one mission: 50 years of Singapore education. http://www.moe.gov.sg/publications/many-pathways.

Ministry of Education, Singapore (2011a). Secondary school education. http://www.moe.gov.sg/education/secondary.

Ministry of Education, Singapore (2011b). Education statistics digest 2011. http://www.moe.gov.sg/education/education-statistics-digest.

Ministry of Education, Singapore (2012a). Gifted education programme: Integrated programme. http://www.moe.gov.sg/education/programmes.

Ministry of Education, Singapore (2012b). School information service (SIS). http://www.app.sis.moe.gov.sg/schinfo.

Ministry of Finance, Singapore (2010). Budget highlights financial year 2010. http://www.news.gov.sg/public/sgpc/en/media-releases/agencies/mof/press-release.

Ng, EH (2011a). Social mobility — the Singapore story: Past, present and future FY 2011. Committee of Supply Debate, 9 March. Available at http://www.moe.gov.sg/medin.speeches/2011/03/07/fy-2011-committee-at-supply-de-l.php.

Ng, IYH (2007). Intergenerational income mobility in Singapore. *The B.E. Journal of Economic Analysis & Policy (Topics),* 7(2), 1–33. http://www.bepress.com/cgi.

Ng, IYH (2011b). Singapore education system: growing worry of social immobility. *The Straits Times,* 16 February.

Ng, IYH (2012). The political economy of intergenerational mobility in Singapore. *International Journal of Social Welfare.* doi: 10.1111/j.1468-2397.2012.00887.x.

Ng, IYH, X Shen and KW Ho (2009). Intergenerational earnings mobility in Singapore and the United States. *Journal of Asian Economics,* 20(2), 110–119. doi: 10.1016/j.asieco.2008.09.010.

Organization for Economic Co-operation and Development (2010). PISA 2009 results: Overcoming social background — equity in learning opportunities and outcomes (volume II), OECD, Paris. http://www.oecd.org/pisa/pisaproducts/pisa2009resultsovercomingsocialbackgroundequityinlearningopportunitiesandoutcomesvolumeii.htm.

Pekkarinen, T, R Uusitalo and S Kerr (2009). School tracking and intergenerational mobility: Evidence from the Finnish comprehensive school reform. *Journal of Public Economics,* 93(7–8), 965–973. doi: 10.1016/j.jpubeco.2009.04.006.

Solon, G (2004). A model of intergenerational mobility variation over time and place. In *Generational Income Mobility in North America and Europe,* M Corak (ed.), pp. 38–47. Cambridge: Cambridge University Press.

Sirkku, K, J Hautamaki and T Karjalainen (2009). *The Finnish Education System and PISA.* Helsinki, Finland: Ministry of Education Publications.

Tan, J (2010). Education in Singapore: Sorting them out? In *Management of Success: Singapore Revisited*, T Chong (ed.), pp. 288–309. Singapore: Institute of Southeast Asian Studies.

Toh, K (2012). Parents renting their way to popular schools. *The Straits Times*, 7 August.

Wong, T (2012). Perceptions about neighbourhood schools must change. *The Straits Times*, 8 March.

World Economic Forum (2012). Global Competitiveness Report 2011–12. Available at www.weforum.org/does/WER_GCR_Report_2011–12.pdf.

Yip, CS (2012). *Intergenerational Income Mobility in Singapore*. Singapore: Ministry of Finance. http://www.app.mof.gov.sg/data/cmsresource. http://www.app.mof.gov.sg/ig-income-mobility.aspx.

CHAPTER 4

RETIREMENT FUNDING AND ADEQUACY

Retirement Funding Adequacy in Singapore

SPEAKER: ASSOCIATE PROFESSOR HUI WENG TAT
Lee Kuan Yew School of Public Policy, National University of Singapore

1. INTRODUCTION

The Asian Financial Crisis in 1997 ended two decades of exuberant growth in the region and ushered in a period of harsher economic reality for Singapore. Rapid technological change and globalization have resulted in major structural changes in Singapore's economy. In the first part of this paper,[1] we will identify the trends that have emerged in the Singapore labor market in the area of employment, productivity growth and unemployment and their implications for job security and employability of the workforce. Following this, we will analyze the efficacy and viability of our current asset-based social security system in providing the retirement needs of the retired workforce. Through simulations, we will examine how existing policies on contributions and withdrawals will affect the ability of the Central Provident Fund (CPF) scheme to adequately provide for retirement. Interventions that will be needed to enhance retirement adequacy and their implications for wage and housing policies will be presented in this paper.

---

[1] A large part of this first section is drawn from the analysis presented in Hui (2011).

2. MACROECONOMIC TRENDS IN THE SINGAPORE LABOR MARKET

An examination of the average growth rate of total employment and real gross domestic product (GDP) over the 1980–2010 period (see Table 1) reveals an increasing tendency toward economic growth that is driven by expansion of employment. This is evident in the employment share of growth, which increased from 31% in the 1980s to 52% in the 1990s and 75% in the 2000s.

A sectoral analysis of labor productivity growth (see Table 2) shows the manufacturing productivity share of growth rising in the 1990s before falling steeply in both share and absolute levels in the last decade.

Service sector employment has displayed strong positive growth since 1986. This expansion of the service sector workforce continued despite negative sectoral growth, recorded during the Asian Financial Crisis in

Table 1. Average Total GDP and Employment Growth (1980–2010).

	1980–1990	1990–2000	2000–2010
Average annual real GDP growth	7.8	7.3	5.2
Average annual employment growth	2.4	3.8	3.9
Average implied annual productivity growth	5.5	3.5	1.3

Source: Singapore Department of Statistics, STS database.

Table 2. Average Sectoral GDP and Employment Growth (1980–2010).

	Manufacturing			Construction			Services		
	1980–1990	1990–2000	2000–2010	1980–1990	1990–2000	2000–2010	1980–1990	1990–2000	2000–2010
Average annual real GDP growth	7.3	7.0	4.8	5.5	11.7	2.9	8.4	7.6	5.9
Average annual employment growth	2.0	0.1	2.8	2.6	10.2	2.7	2.7	4.3	4.5
Average implied annual productivity growth	5.3	6.9	2.0	2.9	1.5	0.2	5.6	3.3	1.5

Source: Singapore Department of Statistics, STS database.

1998 and the global recession in 2009. The strong employment growth in the face of weak output growth has meant that labor productivity of the services sector has suffered successive declines over the past three decades from an average of 5.6% per annum in the 1980s down to 1.5% in the 2000s.

Due to the nature of jobs in the construction sector, employment expansion is heavily dependent on significant numbers of primarily unskilled foreign workers and average productivity growth performance is the weakest of the major sectors, falling from 2.9% in the 1980s to 0.2% in the 2000s.

Since 1997, the number of unemployed has persistently outstripped the number of job vacancies, and this gap has been widening over the years (see Fig. 1). The unemployment rate, which averaged around 2.0% in the 1990s, has increased significantly peaking at 5.2% in 2003. The failure to revert to pre-crisis level suggests a shift in the nature of unemployment toward increasing incidence of structural unemployment.

An examination of the share of unemployment by educational level (see Fig. 2) shows that relative to their share of employment, the share of unemployment of those with lower secondary education and below has declined over the past three decades. This is due to the decrease in this group's employment share as well as the relatively favorable market opportunities for them. The share of unemployed with post-secondary/diploma

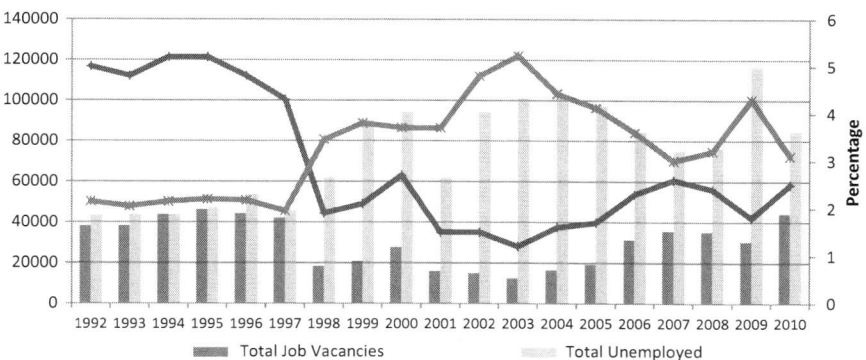

Figure 1. Job Vacancy Rate and Resident Unemployment Rate (1992–2010).
Source: Ministry of Manpower, Labor Market Statistical Information.

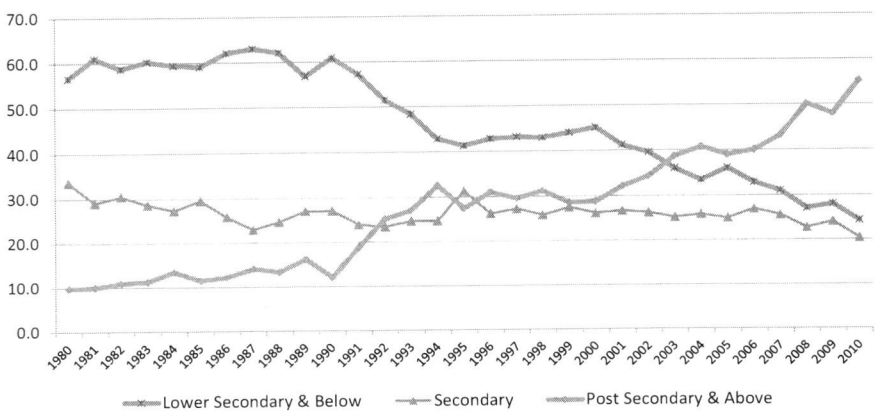

Figure 2. Unemployment Share by Education Level (1980–2010; %).

Source: Reports on labor force in Singapore. Data for 1995 and 2005 are from the General Household Survey; data for 2000 are from the Census of Population.

education and above has seen a significant upward trend over the years. This increase is partly in step with the increasing proportion of employed workers who have attained at least post-secondary/diploma qualifications as well as changes that have taken place in Singapore's immigration policy. The sharp increase in this proportion started from 1990 coinciding with the introduction of a new liberal policy toward foreign skilled labor.

Unemployment among degree holders has also seen a rising trend. The unemployment share of graduates was at a low of 1.8% in 1976 and reached a high of 24.8% in 2009. Even in non-crisis years, there has been an upward trend of graduates being unemployed.

The rising educational level of the unemployed has been accompanied by a significant increase in the share of the unemployed who previously held professional, managers and technicians jobs (see Table 3). This proportion increased from 7.2% in 1976 to 36.2% in 2010 as a result of Singapore's shift in its economic growth strategy to a high-tech value-added manufacturing and rapid expansion of the services sector.

The profile of the retrenched unemployed also indicate a sharp increase in the share of those who possess post-secondary and higher education from 3.1% in 1976 to 51.1% in 2010. Of these, graduates constitute more than half of the retrenched.

Table 3. Profile of Unemployed and Retrenched Workers (1976–2010; %).

	1976	1981	1986	1991	1996	2001	2006	2010
Share of managers, professionals & technicians	7.2	9.4	8.3	14.7	21.9	27.8	30.6	36.2
Share of retrenched unemployed								
In total unemployed	13.0	5.0	25.3	4.8	4.9	19.1	12.8	11.1
With below secondary education	71.9	67.8	63.0	62.8	62.9	50.3	38.0	28.7
With above secondary education	3.1	3.3	7.2	13.9	11.3	24.0	35.0	51.1
With degrees	0	1.6	1.6	7.0	3.2	9.4	18.0	26.6

Source: Report on labor force in Singapore, Ministry of Manpower, various issues.

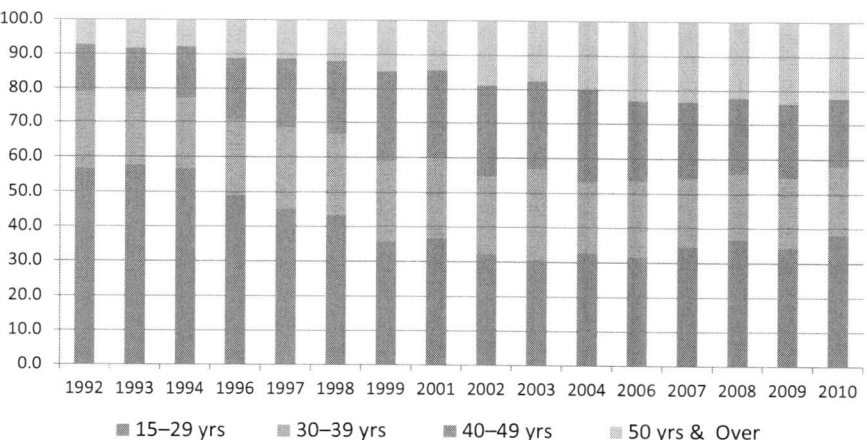

Figure 3. Unemployment Share by Age (1992–2010; %).

Source: Report on labor force in Singapore, Ministry of Manpower, various issues.

The analysis of the age composition of unemployment (see Fig. 3) shows that the share of unemployment in the 15–29 age groups has been falling due to a rise in the number of unemployed older workers. The unemployment share of older workers in the 50 and above age group

Table 4. Average Re-Employment Rate of Retrenched Residents (1997–2010).

Age	97	98	99	00	01	02	03	04	05	06	07	08	08[a]	09[a]	10[a]
Below 30	78.4	68.3	69.9	77.3	73.2	68.4	70.1	73.8	72.2	73.5	76.3	77.4	85.7	77.2	80.8
30–39	72.0	63.9	64.1	69.3	64.4	61.9	63.8	64.7	66.6	71.1	71.9	73.3	82.0	69.9	72.9
40–49	70.0	60.0	60.9	64.2	58.6	59.8	61.6	57.8	62.5	63.7	66.5	70.5	78.4	63.9	67.7
50 & above	58.7	49.9	49.1	52.2	43.1	51.7	56.0	44.7	51.6	58.6	52.0	59.8	68.1	51.7	52.2

Notes: Re-employment rate is defined as the percentage of retrenched who find employment within six months of retrenchment for 1997–2008. From 2008, data refers to those who find employment within 12 months. The data is based on Ministry of Manpower Labor Market Survey and CPF records.
Source: Report on labor force in Singapore, Ministry of Manpower, various issues.

tripled from 7.3% in 1992 to 22.4% in 2010. This is in line with the rising share of older workers aged 50 and above in the workforce, which rose from 12.8% of total employment in 1992 to 26.6% in 2010.

Continued employment of older workers has been difficult especially for those who are retrenched. This difficulty in securing re-employment among older workers is evidenced by the consistently low re-employment rate posted by the older cohort aged 40 years and above (see Table 4), especially following the recession years.

Figure 4 shows the rising shares of older workers in employment and unemployment with the ageing population. The decline in employability of older workers is reflected in the disproportionate increase in their share of unemployment, especially in the periods following economic downturns such as those occurring in 1998, 2001, and 2003. The period following the recent 2008 global recession is uncharacteristic in that share of the older unemployed has not risen. This may be attributed to the existence of employment and wage subsidy schemes, which specifically targeted employment of older workers.

The predicament of older workers in securing employment is evident in their growing share of long-term unemployment in Singapore (see Fig. 5). As expected, long-term unemployment rises significantly after each downturn in the economy. An examination of those long-term unemployed reveals that there is an increasing share of older workers in long-term unemployment. Since the late 1990s, older workers constituted the majority of those in long-term unemployment reaching a peak of 71% in

Retirement Funding and Adequacy 57

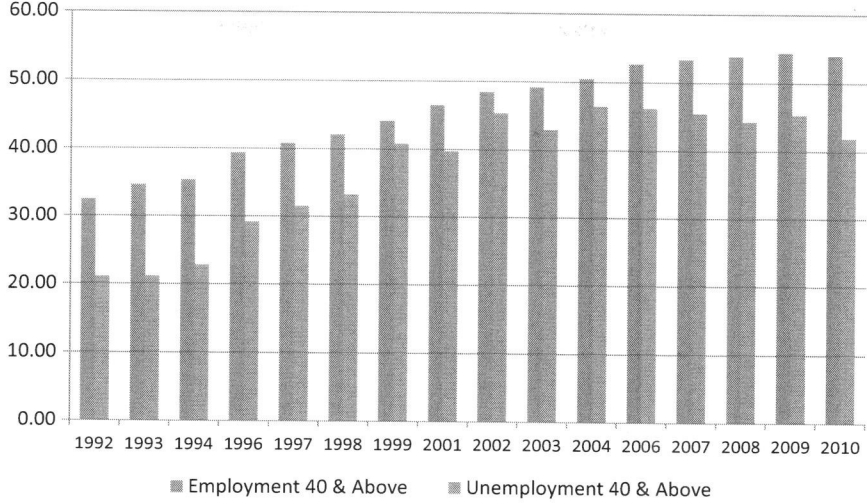

Figure 4. Older Workers in Employment and Unemployment (1992–2010; %).

Note: Data for 1995 are not available, as the Labor Force Survey was not conducted.

Source: Various reports on labor force in Singapore. Data for 1990 and 2000 are from the Census of Population, data for 2005 are from the General Household Survey.

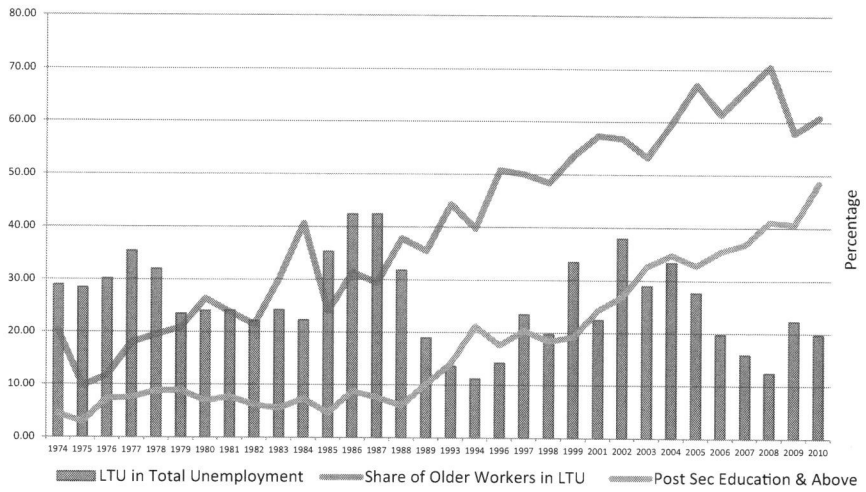

Figure 5. Long-Term Unemployment in Singapore (1974–2010).

Note: Long-term unemployed refers to those who have been unemployed for at least 25 weeks. Data for 1990–1992, 1995, and 2000 are not available.

Source: Various reports on labor force in Singapore, data for 2005 is from the General Household Survey.

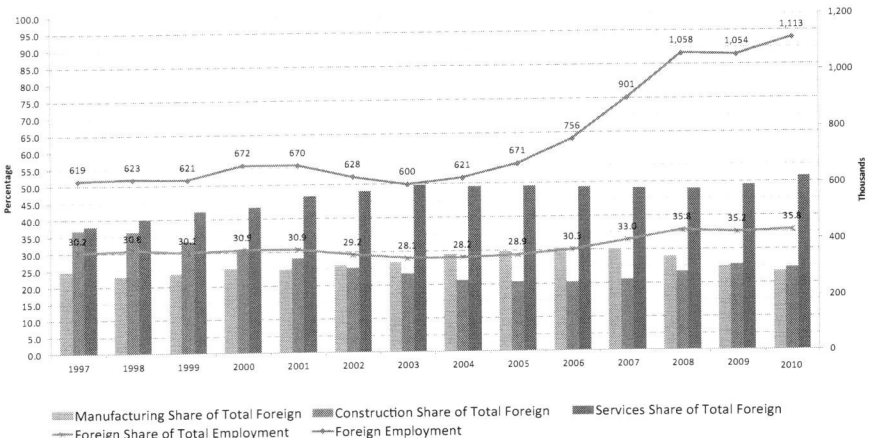

Figure 6. Non-Resident Employment in Singapore (1997–2010).

Source: Labor market, Ministry of Manpower, various issues.

2008. The re-entry of older workers into the workforce thus takes a longer period of time as they often lack the necessary skills and flexibility to move to other industries. Despite the exceptional economic performance of 2007, there was a spike in long-term unemployment in older workers suggesting that older workers are experiencing structural unemployment from changes that make their existing skills obsolete.

Between 1998 and 2010, employed non-residents increased by 494,000, comprising 47% of total new employment created over the period (see Fig. 6). The growing influx of low-skilled, low-cost foreign labor effectively increased overall labor supply dramatically which depressed domestic wages at the bottom of the wage ladder.

The available evidence for this wage depression link is compelling. Over the same period, the estimated real wages of employed residents in the lowest 20% of the wage ladder declined by about 8% while those in the highest 20% of the wage distribution experienced real growth of about 27% (see Fig. 7).

Household income data show a similar uneven distribution of income. The bottom 10% of households share of total incomes has dropped from 2.1 to 1.4% between 1995 and 2010 (see Table 5), while those of top 10% has increased from 31.5 to 36.7% over the same period. The top 10%

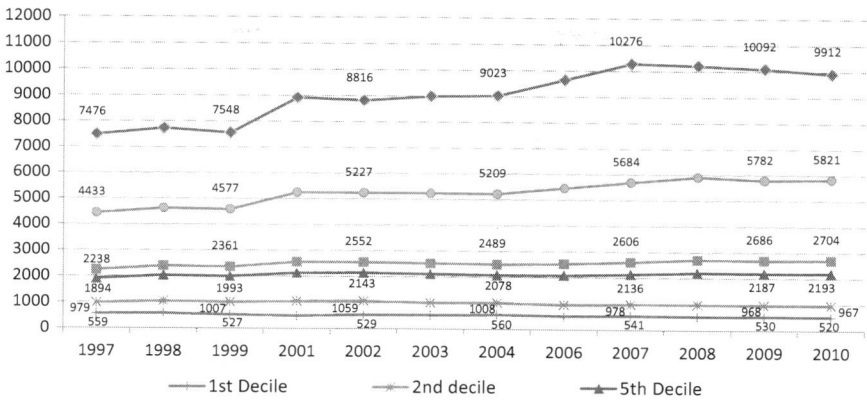

Figure 7. Estimated Real Median Monthly Income of Employed Residents (1997–2010).
Source: Report on labor force in Singapore, Ministry of Manpower, various issues.

Table 5. Income Shares and Ratio of Top and Bottom Deciles.

	1995	2000	2005	2010
Bottom 10% share (%)	2.1	1.8	1.5	1.4
Top 10% share (%)	31.5	33.6	35.4	36.7
Ratio of top to bottom decile	15.3	18.2	23.9	25.9

Source: Key Household Income Trends 2010, Department of Statistics, Singapore.

group is the only income group that has increased its income share over this period. The 81st to 90th group's share has remained steady at 16.2% while all the other deciles' shares have declined.

3. RETIREMENT ADEQUACY OF SINGAPORE WORKFORCE

The adequacy of Singapore's social security system is dependent on buoyant economic growth, increasing real wages and sustained contribution to the CPF. However, with increasing economic uncertainty and volatility, reduced job security and high property prices could undermine the potential efficacy of Singapore's social security system. In this section, we present results of simulations that assess the ability of the CPF system to provide for retirement living.

3.1. Simulation Assumptions

We first examine the income profiles for various groups with differing educational qualifications across the age groups 15–24 years to 50–59 years. Table 6 shows the median gross monthly income from work of full-time employed residents by the various highest qualifications attained. The average annual rates of growth required to reach the median gross income of those in the 50–59 age category are also estimated.

We used these median basic wages[2] and their corresponding growth rates to model the wage growth of three groups of workers with various educational attainments over their working lives.

The conventional measure of retirement adequacy is the income replacement rate (IRR). This is the percentage of pre-retirement working income earnings that individuals can obtain in retirement to maintain their pre-retirement consumption in retirement. The "rule of the thumb" percentage that an individual needs to maintain the same standard of living in retirement is conventionally around 60% to 80%. In this study, an IRR of 66% is set as the target for retirement adequacy.

Total CPF contributions are determined by the age of the person, the corresponding CPF employee and employer CPF contribution rates and the CPF salary ceiling, to which these rates apply. The simulation exercise uses the CPF rates for each age group, as shown in Table 7, which came in force since 1 September 2011.

In the past 25 years, the CPF salary ceiling for contributions has declined from $6,000 in 1985 to its current level of $5000 in 2011 (see Table 8). In our simulations, we first allow for modest increase of $500 per

Table 6. Median Income and Growth Rate by Highest Qualification Attained (2010).

Highest qualification	Basic wage at 22 yrs	Annual growth rate (%)
Secondary and lower sec	$1200	4.1
Post sec	$1500	5.2
Tertiary	$2560	5.9

Source: Report on labor force in Singapore 2010, Ministry of Manpower.

---

[2] The data for wages are inclusive of bonuses received. In our simulations, we have allowed for a more generous assumption by multiplying these basic wages by 13.

Table 7. CPF Contribution Rates (%).

Age	Total	Ordinary account	Special account	Medisave account
Below 35 yrs	36	23.0	6.0	7.0
35–45	36	21.0	7.0	8.0
45–50	36	19.0	8.0	9.0
50–55	30	13.0	8.0	9.0
55–60	21.5	11.5	1.0	9.0
60–65	14	3.5	1.0	9.5
65+	11.5	1.0	1.0	9.5

Source: CPF Board.

Table 8. Changes in Monthly Income Ceiling (1971–2011).

Year of change	OA monthly income ceiling	Real OA monthly income ceiling (in 2010 $)	Total CPF contribution rate (%)	Maximum nominal CPF contribution	Maximum real monthly contribution (in 2010 $)
1971	$1500	$4724	20	$300	$945
1975	$2000	$4108	30	$600	$1232
1978	$3000	$5864	33	$990	$1935
1984	$5000	$7372	50	$2500	$3686
1985	$6000	$8792	50	$3000	$4396
2004	$5500	$6251	33	$1815	$2063
2005	$5000	$5693	33	$1650	$1879
2006	$4500	$5052	33	$1485	$1667
2011	$5000	$4753	36	$1800	$1711

Source: Singapore Yearbook of Manpower Statistics, various issues.

decade and examine the implications on the IRR using an annual inflation rate of 3% and annual growth of wages prevailing in 2010 for the various starting income levels.

In 2010, the average life expectancy at birth was 79 for men and 84 for women, and the average life expectancy at age 65 was 20 years. In the simulation, it is assumed that at the point of retirement, a person is expected to live till age of 85. He or she will use the CPF Ordinary Account (OA) and Retirement Account (RA) savings to purchase a 20-year annuity at 4% return that pays till age 85. The IRR is computed based on the income stream from this annuity.

Other assumptions that have been incorporated in the simulations are:

1. The CPF Minimum Sum is kept at $120,000 (in 2003 dollars) or $140,350 (in 2011 prices). Any OA contribution in excess of the Minimum Sum will be transferred to the Special Account (SA).
2. The Medisave Contribution Ceiling (MCC), is fixed at $5000 above the Medisave Minimum Sum (MMS) of $36,000 at 2011 prices. Any Medisave contribution in excess of the MMC will be transferred to the SA for members below 55 years old.
3. Rates of return on CPF balances are 2.5% p.a. for OA and 4% p.a. for the SA, MA, and RA. An additional 1% interest p.a. is paid on the first $60,000 on combined CPF balances with up to $20,000 from the OA.
4. Earnings are reduced by 10% at the age of 62.

3.2. Simulation Results

The simulation results in Table 9 show that CPF savings at existing contribution rates will be adequate for retirement living at age 65 for those in the lowest wage category. However, for those who earn a median wage and above at age 24, the IRR at age 65 is between 33% to 39%, pointing to retirement inadequacy.

In real terms (in 2010 prices), the value of the monthly CPF salary ceiling has not changed over the past four decades. As shown in Table 8, it was $4724 in 1971 and $4753 in 2011. In between these years, the real income ceiling rose steadily to $8960 before dropping by 47% to its current value of $4753 in 2011. Correspondingly, the maximum CPF contribution in real terms has increased from $935 to $4396 before declining by 61% to $1711 in 2011.

4. INFLATION-ADJUSTED CPF CONTRIBUTION CEILING

OA income ceiling is inflation-adjusted and maintained at its real level in 2011 to show the impact on IRR (see Table 10).

Table 9. IRRs at Retirement Age.

With OA income ceiling rising by $500 per decade			
	Retirement Age		
Basic Starting Salaries	55 yr	60 yr	65 yr
$1200	54.5%	65.0%	85.3%
$1800	47.6%	52.8%	64.6%
$2560	33.0%	34.1%	39.4%
Expected Real Wage (in 2010 prices) at retirement			
	55 yr	60 yr	65 yr
$1200	$1704	$1797	$1705
$1500	$3013	$3349	$3350
$2560	$6400	$7353	$7603

Table 10. Replacement Rates at Retirement with Real CPF Salary Ceiling at 2011 Levels.

Starting salaries	55 yr (%)	Change (%)	60 yr (%)	Change (%)	65 yr (%)	Change (%)
A: $1200	56.5	0.0	67.5	0.0	88.7	0.0
B: $1500	50.3	1.4	58.0	3.5	72.9	6.1
C: $2560	44.8	10.7	48.1	12.8	56.9	16.0

If the CPF salary ceiling is inflation-adjusted and is kept at its real level of $5000 in 2011, there will be significant improvement in the IRR, especially for those in income groups B and C. For those in income group B, the increase in IRR at age 65 is 6.1% while those with median incomes, see an increase of 16%.

A simulation was made to determine the combination of additional increase in CPF salary ceiling increase and the extent of wage increase (relative to base income at 5.9% growth), which would enable retirement adequacy with IRR of 66% to be achieved at age 65 for those in income group C. The results are shown in Table 11.

The results show that further improvement in retirement adequacy for income group C can be achieved through increase in real CPF salary

Table 11. Increase in CPF Salary Ceiling and Wage Growth for Retirement Adequacy.

Increase in real CPF ceiling at 2011 Level	Wage annual growth rate (%)	Increase in wage annual growth rate (%)
$500	10.2	4.3
$750	8.3	2.4
$1000	7.5	1.6
$1250	7.0	1.1
$1500	6.8	0.9

ceiling and higher annual wage growth. If salary ceiling is increases by $500, there needs to be an additional 4.3% growth in wages to enable those in income group C to achieve retirement adequacy at age 65. However, if the salary ceiling is increased by $1000, the additional annual wage increase required is only 1.6%.[3]

5. INCREASE IN TOTAL CPF CONTRIBUTION RATE

How much must CPF contribution rates increase to attain retirement adequacy? The impact of a 1% increase in total CPF contribution rate on the IRR (with inflation-adjusted salary ceiling) is presented in Table 12.

The IRR for those in income group C is increased by 1.2% to 1.5%. To ensure retirement adequacy at age 65, the total contribution rate would have to increase by almost 6%.

6. EFFECT OF PROPERTY PURCHASE ON RETIREMENT ADEQUACY

Thus far, the analyses assume that there are no withdrawals of CPF savings for housing or other investments. We will next examine the impact of housing purchase on retirement adequacy based on the assumption that

---

[3] Further increase in the salary ceiling will have diminishing impact on IRR for those earning around the median income levels because their incomes would not rise fast enough to take advantage of the higher salary contribution ceiling.

Table 12. Effect of 1% Rise in CPF Contribution Rate on IRR.

Starting salaries	With Real CPF salary ceiling at 2011 levels					
	55 yr (%)	Change (%)	60 yr (%)	Change (%)	65 yr (%)	Change (%)
A: $1200	53.3	2.0	63.7	2.5	83.5	3.5
B: $1500	48.4	1.3	55.9	1.6	70.3	2.2
C: $2560	43.9	1.1	47.2	1.2	55.9	1.5

Table 13. Effect of Purchase of the HDB Property on Retirement Adequacy.

Starting salary	HDB price paid	55 yr (%)	60 yr (%)	65 yr (%)
With OA income ceiling raised by $500 per decade				
$1200	$230,000	33.4	40.9	56.7
$1500	$310,000	31.5	35.4	45.0
$2560	$560,000	19.3	19.7	22.4
With OA income ceiling kept constant at 2011 levels				
$1200	$230,000	3.4	40.9	56.7
$1500	$310,000	32.8	38.9	51.1
$2560	$560,000	30.0	32.5	38.4

the CPF contributor enters into a joint purchase agreement with his/her spouse at age 30 in purchasing a property from the Housing and Development Board (HDB), where the mortgage repayment is funded entirely by CPF contributions. The price of the HDB housing indicated is the maximum price that could be supported by the CPF contributions at age 30. This worked out to be around $260,000, $310,000 and $560,000 for those with basic salaries of $1200, $1500 and $2560, respectively at age 22. Loans are taken over a 30-year period at the HDB lending rates of 2.6%.

If CPF salary increases by $500 per decade, the housing purchase will lead to a fall in the IRR of between 17% and 28% at age 65 (see Table 13). With inflation-adjusted CPF salary ceiling, a similar fall in IRR is experienced.

The effect of housing purchase on the IRR at various income levels is illustrated in Fig. 8. The assumption made here is that mortgage

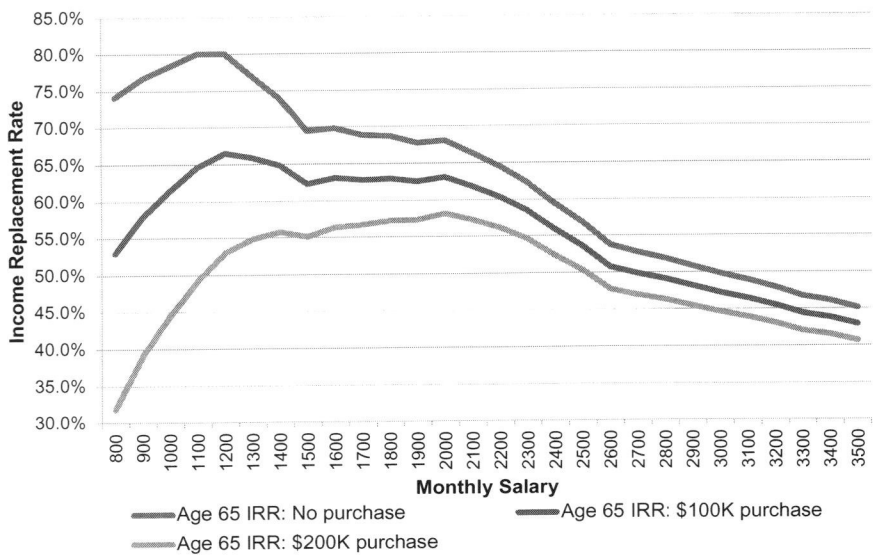

Figure 8. Effect of Housing Purchase on the IRR.

repayment is shared jointly by both working spouses. The effect of housing purchase on the retirement adequacy of a single income household is therefore much greater. If only one spouse is working and shouldering the burden of the housing purchase, the effect of a $100,000 housing price on the IRR would be doubled — equivalent to that shown for the $200,000 purchase shown in the chart.

The impact of housing price increase and the required increase in annual wage growth to offset such IRR falls are shown in Table 14.

Every $100,000 increase in housing prices will reduce the replacement ratios by 3.0% to 12.4%. This would require compensating real wage growth of 0.4% to 1.2% per annum to restore IRR to its original level.

7. EFFECT OF UNEMPLOYMENT ON RETIREMENT ADEQUACY

We analyze the impact of job displacement on the IRR, by assuming one very short episode of unemployment at age 40 and another at age 50. For each episode of job displacement, we assumed that the worker

Table 14. Impact of Property Price Increase and Required Wage Offsets.

Starting salary	Increase in housing price	Fall in IRR with CPF real income ceiling at 2011 levels			Annual wage growth to offset IRR fall (%)
		55 yr (%)	60 yr (%)	65 yr (%)	
$1200	$50,000	−4.6	−5.3	−6.2	0.3
$1500	$50,000	−2.6	−2.8	−3.2	0.2
$2560	$50,000	−1.2	−1.3	−1.5	0.6
$1200	$100,000	−9.2	−10.5	−12.4	0.6
$1500	$100,000	−5.2	−5.6	−6.3	0.4
$2560	$100,000	−2.5	−2.6	−3.0	1.2

Table 15. Effect of Unemployment on Retirement Adequacy.

One unemployment episode		IRR at retirement age		
Starting salary	HDB price paid	55 yr (%)	60 yr (%)	65 yr (%)
A: $1200	$230,000	27.7	33.4	46.5
B: $1500	$310,000	27.4	32.0	42.2
C: $2560	$560,000	27.2	29.9	35.6
Two unemployment episodes				
A: $1200	$230,000	26.2	30.6	42.2
B: $1500	$310,000	25.9	29.4	38.4
C: $2560	$560,000	25.9	28.2	33.7

experiences a wage reduction of 20%. The results in Table 15 show that one bout of job displacement at age 40 will reduce the IRR by 3% to 10% at age 65, with greater reduction for those earning lower income. A second episode of job displacement at age 50 will reduce the IRR by another 2% to 4%.

68 Inequality in Singapore

8. ANNUAL WAGE GROWTH NEEDED TO ACHIEVE RETIREMENT ADEQUACY

The base model assumes annual nominal wage growth as indicated in Table 6. A simulation was conducted to ascertain the annual rate of growth in nominal wage that will enable workers with housing purchase to achieve replacement ratio of 66% at age 65.

The results in Table 16 show that for the lower income groups that do not spend a large amount on housing purchase, the additional annual wage growth required varies from 0.8% (for those who purchase HDB at $230,000) to 10.8% (for those who purchase HDB at $310,000).[4] With real CPF income ceiling kept at 2011 level, the required increases are reduced.

9. INCREASE IN CPF RETURNS ON RETIREMENT ADEQUACY

The next simulation exercise examines how much the CPF rate of return must be increased to achieve retirement adequacy. We determine the levels to which both OA and SA rates would have to be set to achieve an IRR of 66% (Table 17).

Table 16. Required Annual Wage Growth for Retirement Adequacy.

Starting salary	HDB price paid	CPF income ceiling raised by $500 per decade		Real CPF income ceiling kept at 2011 level	
		Annual wage growth	Increase	Annual wage growth	Increase
A: $1200	$230,000	4.90%	0.8%	4.6%	0.5%
B: $1500	$310,000	16.0%	10.8%	6.1%	0.9%
C: $2560	$560,000	unattainable		unattainable	

---

[4]For the higher income category, no amount of increase in wages could enable the desired replacement ratio to be attained. The best that could be achieved was an IRR of 25%, which required an unrealistic 16.5% increase in wage growth. This may be attributed to the low-income ceiling for CPF contributions, which places a limit on the rate of accumulation of CPF savings for retirement. Even with real CPF income ceiling maintained at 2011 levels, it has been found that the maximum IRR attainable was 46%, which required an unrealistically high growth of 20%.

Table 17. Required Returns on CPF Savings to Achieve Retirement Adequacy.

Starting salary at age 22	HDB price paid	CPF OA & SA rate of return to achieve IRR of 66% at age 65			
		Gradual increase in CPF salary ceiling (%)	Constant real income ceiling at 2011 level (%)	Increase of $500 in real salary ceiling (%)	Increase of $1000 in real salary ceiling (%)
A: $1200	$230,000	4.1	4.1	4.1	4.1
B: $1500	$310,000	5.0	4.6	4.6	4.6
C: $2560	$560,000	7.1	5.6	5.4	5.2

Retirement adequacy can be attained for those in income group A with increase in CPF rate of return of 4.1% for both OA and SA accounts. However, for those in the higher income groups who had purchased housing in excess of $300,000, the increase in CPF rates of return would be significantly higher.

The results show that even if CPF real salary ceiling were to be increased by $1000, it would require a significantly larger rate of CPF returns to achieve retirement adequacy. The huge amount of CPF savings, that have been withdrawn for mortgage loan repayments have substantially and adversely affected a large majority of the income groups from achieving retirement adequacy.

10. CONCLUSION

The macroeconomic trends in the Singapore's labor market show that the unemployment rate has climbed a notch higher in past decade. There has also been an inversion of the educational profile of the unemployed — with the more highly educated comprising an increasing share of the unemployed. Older workers are also shouldering a dominant share of total unemployment and an increasing majority share of the long-term unemployed.

These labor market trends in Singapore point to the need to re-strategize our economic growth plans and to rethink of policies that have significant impact on the welfare of the resident workforce. In particular, as older workers are set to become an increasingly important component of the ageing population, there is a need to re-look at policies that will have an impact on the future retirement adequacy of these workers.

Current CPF rates will provide adequate savings for retirement living at age 65 for those in the lower income groups. However, this happens only if there are no withdrawals for housing or other investments. The existing CPF system has been shown to be unable to adequately provide for the retirement needs of a large majority of the resident workforce, especially the growing share of those with tertiary education in the workforce. For this group, even if the contribution income ceiling were to be inflation-adjusted and maintained at the current real level, CPF savings is still inadequate to provide for retirement living. One contributor to the present predicament is the falling real value of CPF contributions since 1985. The increased incidence of displacement of older workers will further aggravate retirement inadequacy. Our analysis has shown that a combination of increases in CPF real salary ceiling, CPF contribution rate and rate of return on CPF savings is needed to rectify the situation. For those in this higher income group, if the CPF real salary ceiling is kept constant, a 6% increase in total contribution rate will be needed to achieve retirement adequacy. Even with the real CPF salary ceiling raised by $1000, an additional 1.6% increase in wage growth or a 5.1% rate of return on CPF savings will be required.

Property price escalation poses a serious threat to retirement adequacy. The consequential wage increases needed to restore retirement adequacy will have adverse implications for wage competitiveness and increased pressure on the need for greater productivity growth. In view of this, there is a need to continue to contain, if not deflate property prices for long-term sustainability of the economy. Hence, a strategic review of longer-term impact of policies on property price and future welfare of residents is overdue, and this will require a move away from promoting property as an investment to using property primarily for consumption purposes. Unlike other countries that have significant land resources, Singapore should not rely on property investment act as a catalyst for economic growth. Lower property prices will not only prevent more resources to be diverted from welfare-enhancing consumption, but also allow adequate resources to be set aside for retirement living in the future.

The link between property price escalation and its adverse impact on retirement adequacy and wage competitiveness must be recognized in policy decisions regarding the HDB property prices. In addition, if property prices are made more affordable and the resulting pressures on the need for dual income families are considerably lessened as a consequence, it will produce a more conducive environment for raising fertility rates in the longer term.

11. COMMENTS ON PRESENTATION BY SPEAKER

Discussant: Mr Chan Beng Seng

Divisional Director, Ministry of Manpower

11.1. Comments on the Model and Analysis

My comments will be in four parts. First, on how the IRR is modeled; second, the role of CPF; third, the role of housing in retirement adequacy; and finally, employment among older workers.

11.1.1. *IRR model*

IRR is a simple concept, but generating an estimate is more complex than it first appears. First, we must make a choice of data to use, and associated with this is the availability of data. Second, it also involves an element of judgment.

Considering these challenges, I think Prof. Hui's analysis is a commendable effort. I am somewhat familiar with the challenges, as we have also developed estimates of the IRR in-house. Let me share with you one example of each type of challenge.

First, deciding what data to use. Let us consider income growth. Income is typically modeled by assuming a constant wage growth. This is what the Organization for Economic Co-operation and Development (OECD) does, and it is also what the Prof. Hui has done. However, in reality, a person's income does not rise at a constant rate as he or she ages. It rises very fast when a person is young, and slows down as one ages.

In the context of retirement adequacy, this is very important because greater savings at a younger age has a powerful effect, due to compounding interest. Our own analysis shows that this difference in income growth modeling can change IRR estimates by more than 10%.

Second, the role of judgment. Let me use an example that is again related to income data. The denominator of the IRR formula is the income that we seek to replace. What income level should this be? Should it be average lifetime income? Should it be last drawn income?

Prof. Hui has used last-drawn income. Since the income growth assumption used in his model is a constant growth over a person's working career, this means the last drawn income is pretty high. Should a person in retirement expect to replace half or two-third of the income earned at his or her peak, or some other lower level of income?

Just as an illustration of how large this could impact the results, if the model presented had used average real income instead of the last drawn income, the IRR would have increased by 5%–10%.

There is no clear best method to do this. It is a matter of opinion. But it does demonstrate how judgment on what is appropriate can affect IRR estimates significantly.

I have shared just two examples, but I hope they help illustrate that, to interpret what an IRR number means, one has to be aware of how the number was derived.

11.1.2. *Role of the CPF*

Let me move on to the role the CPF should play in retirement adequacy. Prof Hui's analysis leads him to be concerned about the CPF's ability to provide for retirement adequacy for the better educated — essentially those with higher incomes, and perhaps those with middle incomes too.

This is also a matter we study at the Ministry of Manpower. Our primary approach for evaluating retirement adequacy is attainment of the Minimum Sum, which is an estimate of what is required to attain a modest standard of living in retirement. But we also estimate the IRR that the CPF can deliver.

We base our IRR model on empirical data as far as possible, so as to minimize subjectivity. For example, how long should we assume a person does not work and therefore does not contribute to his income? We base it on what we find in CPF records.

Our analysis shows that the IRR for a median income earner is about two-thirds. This is after the median earner has purchased a home.

Now, an IRR of about two-thirds is comparable to that for median earners in OECD. Two-thirds is a level that many would consider satisfactory, including Prof. Hui, I believe. We therefore are of the view that the CPF caters adequately for the middle income.

Prof. Hui's analysis gives a somewhat lower IRR. As my earlier examples show, it is pretty easy for the various differences in model details to result in such differences. So to which number should you refer? As I mentioned, you need to know the assumptions used and decide for yourself. For that reason, we are planning to issue a paper with details of how we model IRR in a few months' time.

However, we do have some common findings. Similar to Prof. Hui, we find that the IRR for lower-income Singaporeans would be higher, as should be the case since, considering their lower income, they need a higher IRR in retirement. We also find that higher-income Singaporeans will have lower IRR; it gets lower, the higher the income becomes.

Prof. Hui's model shows that IRR for the tertiary educated would be about 40%, after a home is purchased. In absolute terms, this would be a stream of income higher than what a median earner, for instance, would receive. Whether this is enough depends on the expectations of the individual.

However, it is reasonable to assume that many higher-income individuals would like a higher level of expenditure in retirement. In practice, what happens is that this higher-income person would typically also have private savings to supplement own savings, attaining a higher total IRR in that way.

We could make a case for CPF savings alone to be sufficient in providing higher-income individuals with a high IRR. However, this means contributing more in the CPF. Not everyone will welcome this. And there are downsides. For instance, those with lower-incomes might over-save, reducing their take-home pay.

So we have designed the CPF to meet modest retirement needs. We think higher-income Singaporeans are able to save more for themselves outside of the CPF; and believe many would prefer to save on their own too.

11.1.3. *Role of housing*

Prof. Hui is of the view that we should move to a model where we do not depend on investment in housing to attain retirement adequacy.

I agree with him. In our own in-house modeling, we assume that a person buys a home within his means, and stays in it for life without moving to a smaller flat in retirement.

Prof. Hui points out the importance of reining in expenditure on property so as to ensure prudent use of CPF savings. This is also an important point. If a person buys a property beyond his means, he may have to be prepared to move to a smaller flat in retirement. And we need property prices to be kept in check. The Ministry of National Development (MND) is certainly trying its best to do so.

While we should aim not to rely on housing investment to attain retirement adequacy, it is a good fall-back — an insurance policy so to speak, if a person does not manage to save enough.

This describes some Singaporeans of the older generations, those in their 50s, 60s, and 70s today. They have low cash savings in their CPF. Why is this so? There are a few key reasons:

First, incomes were much lower in the past. In the case of women, many did not work consistently, if they worked at all. Second, we allowed more CPF savings to be withdrawn at age 55 in the past. Third, we allowed a larger proportion of CPF savings to be used for housing, as the priority was to raise our then low rates of home ownership.

Those Singaporeans who have low savings in their CPF would supplement it with private savings, or receive support from their families. About two-thirds of those aged 65 and above receive a monthly allowance from family.

With much of their CPF savings in housing, these older Singaporeans can also unlock their savings if they need. They can sublet a room, move to a smaller flat and benefit from the recently announced Silver Housing Bonus, or sell the tail end of their lease back to the HDB via the lease buyback scheme, which was recently enhanced.

So, yes, we should not plan for housing investment to provide for retirement, but I would still give it a role — a role that kicks in when a particular individual finds that his cash savings proves to be insufficient.

11.1.4. Work among older workers

Prof. Hui is concerned that older workers face greater difficulty in remaining in the workforce, and that this would aggravate retirement adequacy.

Such a conclusion cannot be drawn from the data. His slides show a rising share of older workers among the unemployed. These are explained by compositional shifts in the labor force.

The data we should be looking at is the labor force participation rate and unemployment rate among older workers. Labor force participation rate for older workers has been rising. Unemployment rate among older workers have not worsened compared to younger workers (see Table 18 and Fig. 9). So more older people are working today. The trends are in favor of improving retirement adequacy, not less.

And with the re-employment legislation now in force, and the enhanced Special Employment Credit (SEC), which pays employers up to 8% of income for hiring workers aged 50 and above, we can look forward

Table 18. Resident Unemployment Rate (Annual Average) by Age; 2001, 2006 and 2011.

Age	Unemployment rate (%)		
	2001	2006	2011
Total	3.7	3.6	2.9
Below 30	5.1	5.4	5.0
30–39	3.1	3.0	2.4
40–49	3.4	3.0	2.1
50 & Over	3.5	3.4	2.5

Note: Annual figures are the simple averages of the non-seasonally adjusted unemployment figures obtained at quarterly intervals.
Source: Labor Force Survey, Ministry of Manpower Singapore.

76 Inequality in Singapore

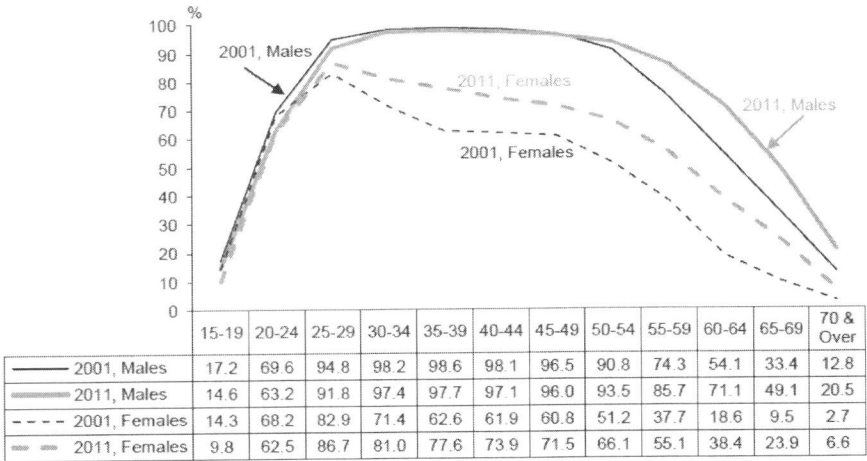

Figure 9. Age-Sex Specific Resident Labor Force Participation Rate, 2001 and 2011.
Source: Labor Force Survey, Ministry of Manpower Singapore.

to a greater number of older workers in the workforce in the future, which will be good for retirement adequacy.

11.2. Concluding Remarks

In conclusion, let me add that the trends for retirement adequacy are positive. As we raise our productivity, income growth would improve and this will mean more retirement savings. As older workers remain in the workforce for longer, they will also be able to save more. The government will of course also continually improve the CPF system from time to time, to ensure that it can cater to the needs of the majority.

REFERENCE

Hui, WT (2011). Employment, unemployment and economic growth: Singapore's experience. Paper presented at the *26th Pacific Economic Community Seminar on Examining the Mid- and Long-Term Structural Unemployment in Asia-Pacific*, 13–14 October. Taipei, Taiwan.

CHAPTER 5

FOREIGN TALENT AND THEIR IMPACT ON THE SINGAPORE ECONOMY

Impact of Foreign Workers on Economic Growth of Singapore Economy

SPEAKER: ASSOC. PROF. SHANDRE M THANGAVELU
*Department of Economics, Faculty of Arts and Social Sciences,
National University of Singapore*

1. INTRODUCTION

Immigrant labor is an important source of human capital to complement and enhance economic growth in an open economy. Recent studies highlight that the inflow of immigrants, especially skilled immigrants, could increase the expected returns on education. There are also positive effects on the host economy in terms of complementing the domestic human capital and increasing the domestic innovation activities (Vidal, 1998; Mountford, 1999; Stark and Wang, 2002; Chander and Thangavelu, 2005). Recent empirical evidence indicates that the productive impact of immigrants depends on their level of skills and the natives, and also on the host economy's domestic productive capacity to "absorb" and complement foreign labor. For example, studies by Borjas *et al.* (2008), Ottaviano and Peri (2008) and Peri and Sparber (2009) show that the effects of immigrants on the domestic economy depend on the skilled characteristics of the native and immigrant workers in the production process. In addition, evidence from the US economy suggests that immigrants increase total factor productivity (TFP) through efficient task specialization in the labor market, but also promote the adoption of low-skilled biased technology due to a large inflow of unskilled workers (Peri, 2009). A study on the UK and Spain highlights different impact of immigrants on the domestic economy, where immigrants have more productive impact in the UK as compared to Spain (Kangasniemi *et al.*, 2008).

Increasingly, the Singapore economy is relying on foreign workers, both skilled and unskilled, to maintain competitiveness and economic growth. Foreign labor is expected to fill the manpower shortage and also maintain the cost competiveness of domestic firms in global trade. Foreign labor, both skilled and unskilled, serves a dual purpose for the small open economy. Given that the Singapore economy is moving to higher value-added activities, it faces strong shortage of skilled domestic workforce to maintain the viability of high-end value-added industries. Economists expect skilled foreign workers to augment domestic human capital and thus induce innovative activities in the domestic economy; this is expected to maintain competitiveness of exports of the local firms in high-end products. In contrast, the economy also attracts low-skilled foreign workers to manage the "hollowing-out" effects of multinationals as they restructure their production structure toward low-cost countries such as India and China. As the "hollowing-out" effects of multinational could create structural unemployment of local workers in the economy — due to the dislocation of the low-end production chain — unskilled foreign workers are seen as one way to keep the cost of production down and manage the dislocation of multinationals in the domestic economy (Chia *et al.*, 2004).

Given the ageing labor force, foreign workers have become an increasingly important component to augment the domestic labor force in Singapore. While foreign workers are necessary to fill the manpower shortage and generate more economic activity, there are concerns raised as to whether the influx of foreign workers has depressed the wages of local workers, particularly that of low-skilled workers, and also affected innovative activities in the domestic economy.

The effects of migration on the equilibrium and dynamics of the labor market is quite complex, given the characteristics of migrants and current domestic economic conditions in the economy. In the short run, inflow of foreign workers could resolve the cyclical fluctuations and short-term shortages of the labor market, thereby maintaining stability of the labor market. In the long run, in addition to augmenting the ageing labor force, the impact on the long-term growth of foreign workers depends on their productivity and hence on their skills and human capital. This will have a direct impact on innovative and technology adoption capability of domestic firms. Thus, the average level of human capital of foreign workers will have long-term implications for the Singapore economy.

In this paper, we study the impact of immigrants on the Singapore economy. The paper studies the key trends of immigrants and productivity growth. The flow of immigrants could have several effects on industrial activities, dependent on the characteristics of foreign workers. Selective immigration policy of allowing skilled foreign workers could complement the returns on new technologies and hence increase the incentives to adopt new technologies. This could potentially increase the skilled-biased technological change, thereby increasing the demand for skilled workers. This will potentially increase the wages of skilled workers relative to unskilled workers. In contrast, unskilled foreign workers could reduce the incentive to adopt new technologies and contribute to the expansion of low value-added activities, thereby affecting industrial competitiveness and overall productivity growth. The paper examines the impact of foreign workers on capital investment and export share of the manufacturing sector.

Recent empirical studies on developed countries provide inconclusive evidence of the impact of immigrants on the host countries. According to Borjas (1999), immigrants could increase the income of the native population in the host country due to lower cost of labor, increase in capital investments and overall productivity improvements from skilled immigrants. However, the magnitude of this "immigration surplus" depends on the differences of skill components between the native and the immigrant workers, and it could reach a maximum level when their production complementarities are fully exploited. Borjas' study highlights that underlying the immigration surplus is a significant redistribution of wealth from the native workers to the employers of the immigrant workers, thereby lowering the wage rate of native workers and widening the wage gap in the labor market.

Drinkwater *et al.* (2007) revisited Borjas' work by calibrating a three-sector general equilibrium model with endogenous growth to the European Union economies. The study highlights that skilled immigrants tend to increase long-term growth by stimulating more skill-intensive research and development activities in the innovative sector. There are gains in growth and the immigration surplus increase further when there is complementarity between skilled workers and physical capital. The study further highlights that unskilled immigration has negative impact on the size of immigration surplus, thereby supporting immigration policies that favor skilled immigrants. Hunt and Gauthier-Loiselle (2008), using the number of patents as a proxy for innovation, show that skilled immigrants (bachelor degree holders, post-graduate degree holders, engineers and scientists) exert positive effect on patent per capita during the 1950–2000 period in the US.

There are several studies on the impact of immigrants on the wage rate of the host economy. In the US, Peri (2009) predicts a 0.5% increase in income per worker as a result of 1% increase in employment due to immigration inflow. In contrast, Borjas (2003, 2009) finds that recent immigration adds downward pressure on the native workforce wages, particularly for unskilled workers. Card (2004) shows that in high-immigration US cities, companies adapt to the relative supply of workers with different skill levels by adjusting their production technology, and there is no significant change in the relative wage rates after immigration. Chang (2002), using a general equilibrium framework for the Taiwanese economy, highlights that the inflow of foreign workers tends to exert a negative impact on the wages of the local unskilled workers, thereby widening the wage gap. A study by Choi (2004) for the Korean economy shows that the positive impact of immigration critically depends on the price flexibility in the economy and there are larger welfare gains if the immigration policy is skill-biased.

2. KEY EMPLOYMENT TRENDS OF RESIDENT AND NON-RESIDENT LABOR FORCE IN SINGAPORE

Since independence, Singapore has adopted an economic development strategy that allows relatively free movement of foreign capital and labor into the economy. In recent years the external environment is exerting strong economic pressures on Singapore to structurally adjust toward the knowledge-based economy to remain globally competitive. Given the lack of local human capital to support these strong pressures, foreign labor force becomes an important component to augment domestic human capital (Tan *et al.*, 2001). Hui and Hashmi (2007) also highlight the growing reliance on immigrants as an important source to augment local population and workforce, due to the declining fertility rate and an ageing population.

The non-resident labor is becoming an important component of the labor force (Fig. 1). Total employment doubled by 2008, increasing from nearly 1.5 million in 1992 to around three million workers, with the share of non-residents rising to nearly 36% of the total employment (Ministry of Manpower, 2008b). The reliance of non-resident as an important component of the labor market is reflected by the strong growth in the post-Asian Financial Crisis. From 1998 to 2002, the non-resident employment showed a declining trend growing at an average rate of only 0.3% in

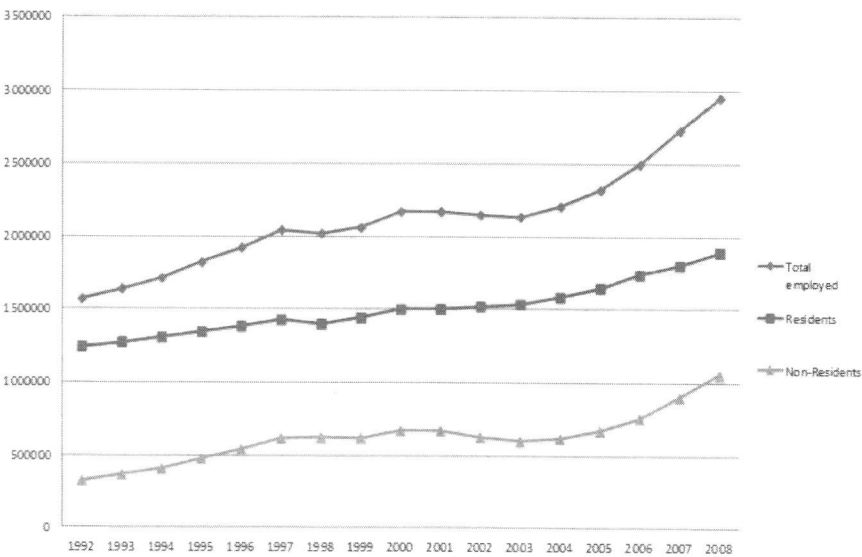

Figure 1. Total Employment by Resident and Non-Resident Labor Force for Singapore From 1992–2008.

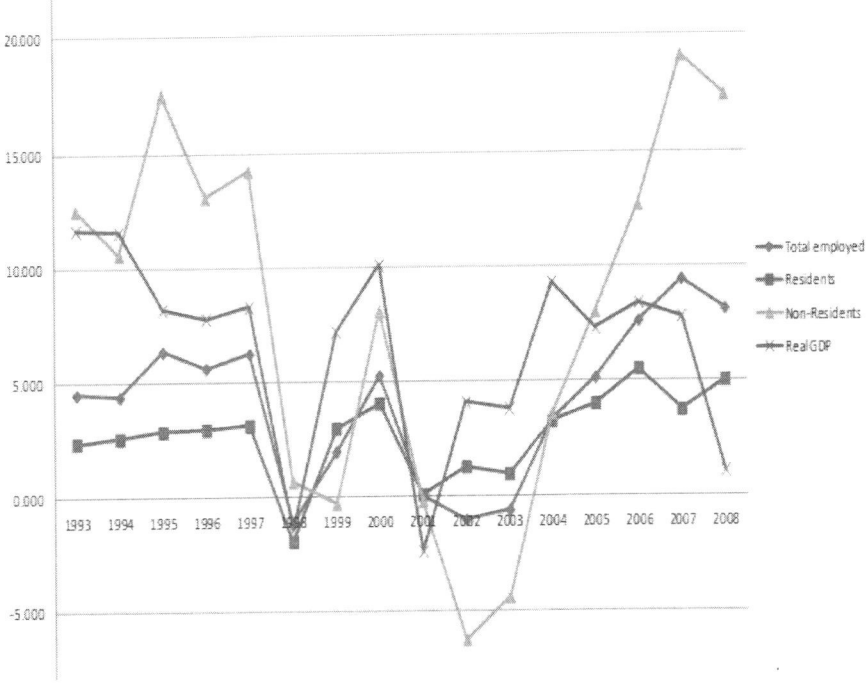

Figure 2. Growth in Real Gross Domestic Product (GDP), Local Employment (Residents and Non-Residents) From 1992–2008.

contrast to the rising trend from 2003 to 2008, where the non-resident employment grew at an annual rate of nearly 9.4%. In the post-Asian Financial Crisis period, resident employment grew by only 3.7% and it was mostly driven by the growth in permanent residents.

3. SECTORAL EMPLOYMENT OF RESIDENT AND NON-RESIDENT LABOR FORCE

The share of employment to total employment by sectors is given in Table 1. The share of manufacturing employment to overall employment accounts for nearly 25% in the pre-Asian Financial Crisis and this declined to around 20% in the post-crisis. This is mainly attributed to the "hallowing-out" effect as key industries in Singapore relocate their production to

Table 1. Share of Employment to Total Employment by Sectors in Singapore From 1992–2008 (%).

	1992–1997	1998–2008	2003–2008
Manufacturing	24.5	20.3	20.4
Resident	14.7	11.9	11.3
Non-Resident	7.5	8.3	8.9
Services	62.2	66.8	68.2
Resident	52.5	52.5	53.2
Non-Resident	10.2	14.4	15.0
Construction	12.5	12.2	10.8
Resident	4.4	4.3	4.1
Non-Resident	8.0	7.9	6.7

Source: Ministry of Manpower, Singapore. Some years are extrapolated based on published data from Ministry of Manpower (2004, 2008a, 2008b, 2009). Thus, there might be rounding-off errors in the data. The above sample is only an approximation from 1992–1996.

countries with lower production costs, and with the manufacturing sector moving to higher value-added production. It is clear from the Table 1 that services is emerging as a strong sector for employment creation and also as a buffer to absorb displaced workers from the manufacturing sector. The share of services employment increased from 62% in 1992–1997 to nearly 67% in 1998–2008. In comparison, the construction sector only accounts for 12% of the total employment at the same time period; furthermore, it is primarily driven by the non-resident employment, accounting for nearly 80% of the construction employment.

3.1. Employment in the Manufacturing Sector

The employment of residents and non-residents for the manufacturing sector is given in Figs. 3 and 4. The rising share of non-residents in the manufacturing employment reflects the importance of foreign labor to drive the manufacturing output in the Singapore economy. In 1992, resident employment accounted for nearly 63% of total employment in the manufacturing sector. This declined to nearly 49% in 2008, with nearly equal share of employment of non-residents. It is very likely that the

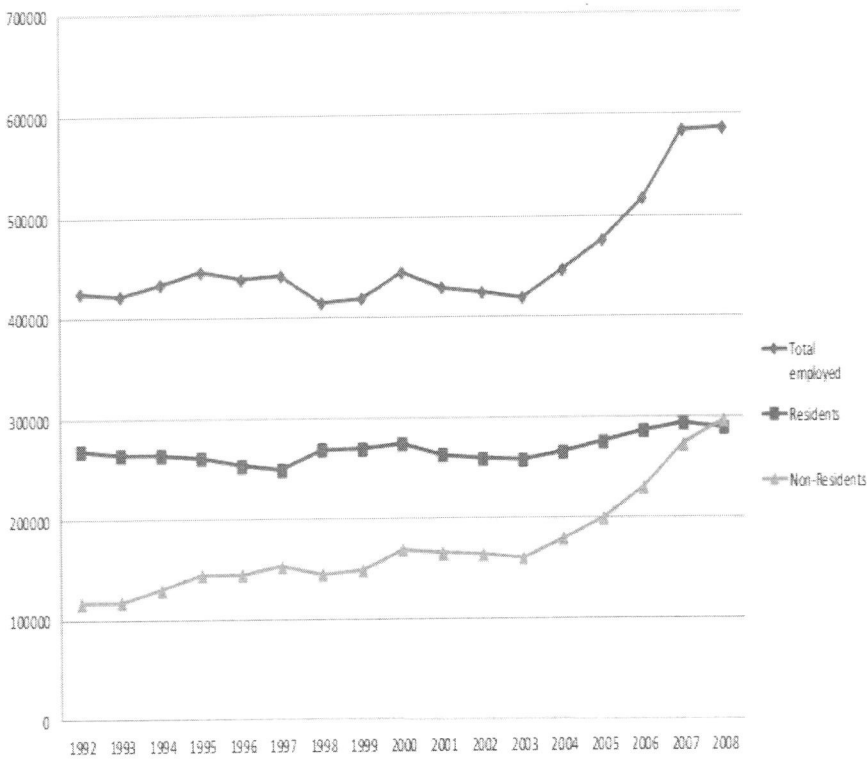

Figure 3. Resident and Non-Resident Labor Force in Manufacturing From 1992–2008.

Source: Ministry of Manpower, Singapore. Some years are extrapolated based on published data from Ministry of Manpower (2004, 2008a, 2008b, 2009). Thus, there might be rounding-off errors in the data. The above sample is only an approximation from 1992–1996.

greater share of skilled workers might be employed in the manufacturing sector given that there was stronger innovation and technology development in this sector.[1]

The strong growth of non-residents in the manufacturing employment is reflected in Fig. 4. We can observe that the annual growth rate of

---

[1] The breakdown of skilled types of foreign workers is not publically available and thus we are not able to decompose the non-resident employment by skill types. In particular, the foreign workers could be classified by their skill type based on the employment. Pass given in terms of employment-pass (EP) for skilled workers, S-pass (SP) for semi-skilled workers, and work-pass (WP) for unskilled workers.

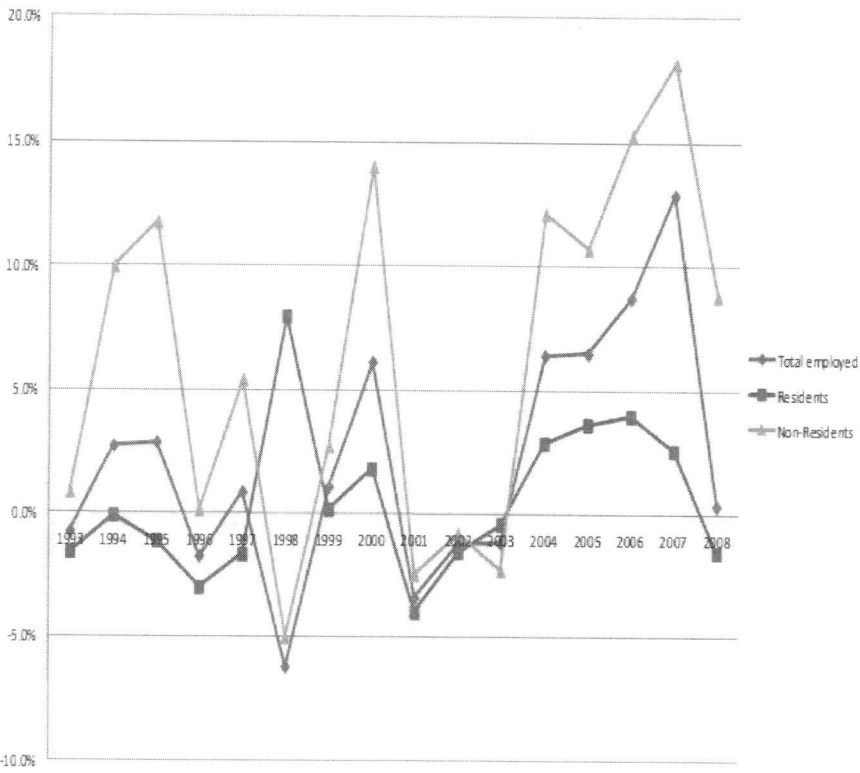

Figure 4. Growth of Total Employment, Local (Residents) and Foreign (Non-Residents) in Manufacturing From 1992–2008.

resident employment was only around 0.5% as compared to nearly 5.6% of the non-resident employment in 1992–2008. The reliance of foreign workers, in particular skilled workers, increased as the manufacturing sector moved into higher value-added activities. This was clearly evident prior to the Asian Financial Crisis. Pre-crisis, non-resident employment grew at an average of 5.6% from 1993–1997, in contrast to a negative 1.4% growth for the resident employment. The employment of non-resident labor force also shows a stronger growth in the post-crisis period of 1998–2008 with an annual rate of nearly 6.4%. In Fig. 4, we can observe a rising trend of non-residents employment in 2002–2008, during the rapid GDP growth period. From 1998 to 2002, non-resident employment shows a declining trend growing at an average rate of only 1.7%. In contrast, we observe a rising trend in 2003–2008, where the non-resident employment grew at an annual rate of nearly 10.5%. In the post-crisis period, resident manufacturing employment grew by only 1.4%; as in the overall employment, it was also driven by the growth in permanent residents.

3.2. Employment in the Services Sector

The employment trends for the services sector are given in Figs. 5 and 6. As compared to the manufacturing sector, the services sector experienced stronger resident employment. On average, resident employment accounted for nearly 80% in 1992–2008. In fact, the services sector tends to play an important role in absorbing and buffering employment growth for resident

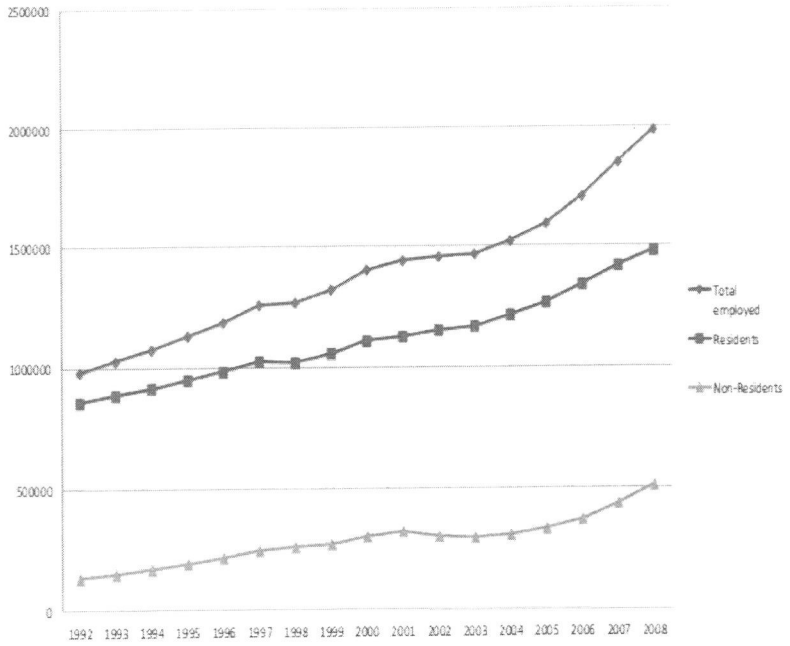

Figure 5. Resident and Non-Resident Labor Force in Services From 1992–2008.

Source: Ministry of Manpower, Singapore. Some years are extrapolated based on published data from Ministry of Manpower (2004, 2008a, 2008b, 2009). Thus, there might be rounding-off errors in the data. The above sample is only an approximation from 1992–1996.

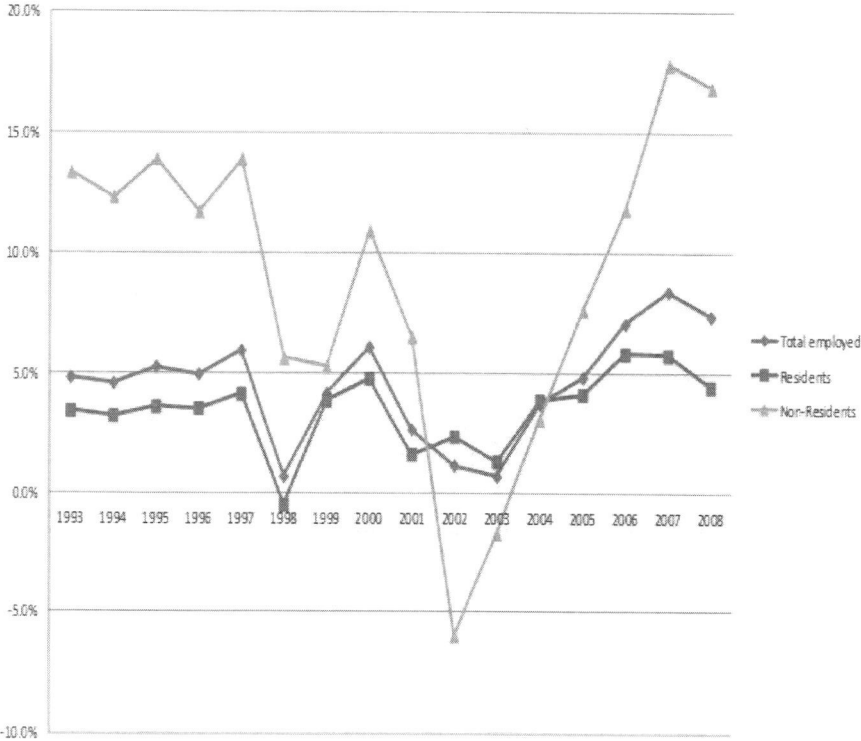

Figure 6. Growth of Total Employment, Local (Residents) and Foreign (Non-Residents) in Services From 1992–2008.

labor force displaced from the manufacturing sector due to structural changes in the economy. However, we do see rising trend of non-resident employment in recent years in the services sector. In 1992, the share of non-resident employment was around 13% and this increased to 26% in 2008.[2]

Compared to the manufacturing sector, resident employment in services grew at a stronger rate of nearly 3.5% in 1992–2008. In fact, we observe a stronger resident employment growth in the post-crisis period; in particular, it grew around 4.2% in 2003–2008. The stronger growth in

---

[2] There are nearly 135,000 foreign domestic workers in Singapore as on 2009, which accounted for around 4.5% of the total employment. This is reflected in the services sector data [(see the Manpower Research and Statistics Department (MRSD) report, labor market 2009)].

the resident employment shows that the services sector was an important buffer for local employment growth in the economy. The non-resident employment also grew at nearly 13% in the pre-crisis period, but declined to around 7.1% in 1998–2008. However, in the more recent period of 2003–2008, we observe a strong non-resident employment growth of nearly 9.3%. This indicates that there had been greater reliance of the services sector for non-resident employment to maintain its growth momentum and greater competition for local employment.

3.3. Employment in the Construction Sector

The employment trends for the construction sector are given in Figs. 7 and 8. Construction sector only accounted for around 12% of the overall employment from 1992–2008, and it is primarily driven by the non-resident

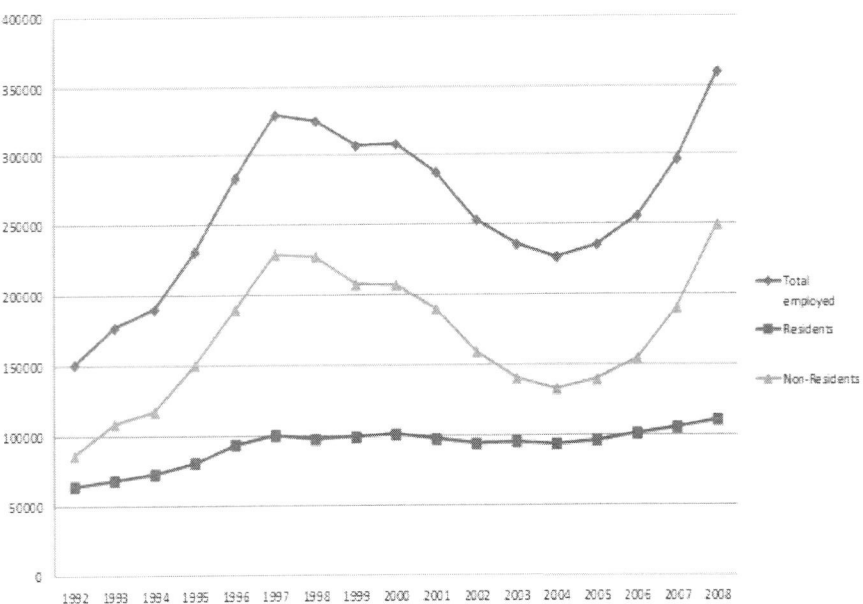

Figure 7. Resident and Non-Resident Labor Force in Construction From 1992–2008.

Source: Ministry of Manpower, Singapore. Some years are extrapolated based on published data from Ministry of Manpower (2004, 2008a, 2008b, 2009). Thus, there might be rounding-off errors in the data. The above sample is only an approximation from 1992–1996.

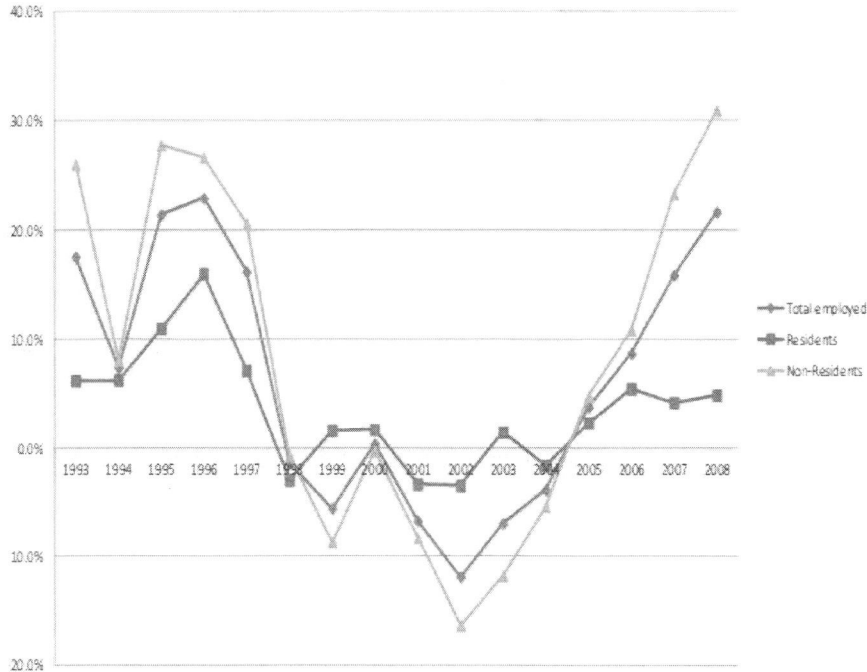

Figure 8. Growth of Total Employment, Local (Residents) and Foreign (Non-Residents) in Construction From 1992–2008.

employment. The foreign labor force accounted for nearly 80% of the total employment of the construction sector. Given the importance of public infrastructure for the Singapore, it is clear that non-resident labor force provides significant contribution to the construction sector and Singapore economy. However, given the large share of unskilled foreign workers (on WP employment) at low wages, there is a greater fragmentation of the industry in terms of allocation of specific task across different construction companies leading to inefficiencies and disincentives to adopt new technologies. Large companies tend to sub-contract specific tasks to smaller companies to reduce the overall cost of operations. In turn, smaller companies tend to complete the sub-contracted work in the least costly and inefficient manner using unskilled foreign workers. The large inflow of unskilled foreign workers tends to increase the incentive to use technologies that are not

90 *Inequality in Singapore*

skill-biased (or labor-intensive) and reduce the incentive for innovation and higher value-added activities. Thus, there is an urgent need to consolidate the construction industry to create greater economies of scale in the industry.

4. CONTRIBUTION OF LOCAL AND FOREIGN LABOR TO GDP

To understand the overall contribution of local and foreign labor force to output growth, we undertake a decomposition of GDP into productivity and employment contributions (see Chia *et al.*, 2004). In Table 2, the GDP growth is decomposed into components attributed to output, labor productivity and growth associated with changes in local and foreign employed manpower.

In 1992–1997, the Singapore economy experienced an average annual GDP growth of around 11.7%, which is well above the economy's potential growth of 4% to 5%. As indicated in Table 2, the growth of foreign labor of around 4.5% is crucial to maintain an average GDP growth rate of 11.7% in 1992–1997. The short-term impact and management of foreign workers are quite visible in the post-crisis period of 1997–2002 as the GDP growth rate decelerated to around 3% due to several negative external shocks such as Severe Acute Respiratory Syndrome (SARS), terrorism and slump in global electronic demand. As GDP growth declined, we also

Table 2. Growth Decomposition in Productivity and Labor Growth From 1992 to 2008 (%).

		GDP	Productivity	Local labor	Foreign labor
1992–1997	Annual average growth	11.7	4.4	2.8	4.5
	Share of growth	100.0	37.2	24.3	38.6
1997–2002	Annual average growth	3.0	2.0	1.0	0.1
	Share of growth	100.0	64.1	32.8	3.1
2002–2008	Annual average growth	6.0	1.5	2.3	2.2
	Share of growth	100.00	24.3	39.0	36.7

Decomposition from 1992–2002 is from Chia *et al.* (2004).

observed foreign labor declining to around 0.1%. This reflects the flexibility and veritable role of foreign labor as a buffer for the overall production structure of the economy. In recent years the contribution of foreign labor to GDP growth has significantly increased. In 2002–2008, foreign labor contribution was 37%, which was nearly equivalent to the contribution of local labor of 39% of GDP growth. This clearly reflects the reliance of foreign human capital for sustained growth of the Singapore economy.

It is interesting to note the importance of labor productivity for Singapore. The contribution of growth in labor productivity in GDP had risen from 37% in 1992–1997 to 64% in 1997–2002, which could be attributed to rising capital intensity and wider use of information technologies. However, in recent years the labor productivity is showing a declining trend. The contribution of labor productivity to GDP growth has declined from 64% in 1997–2002 to only 24% in 2002–2008. This indicates that GDP growth in the recent years is driven more by labor input growth, in particular foreign labor, as compared to growth from capital intensity and innovative activities.

The key objective of the foreign manpower policy is to complement the domestic human capital by allowing skilled foreign workers into the Singapore economy, thereby complementing innovation and technology adoption capacity of domestic firms (Chia *et al.*, 2004). However, the returns on foreign labor critically depend on the industrial structure of the domestic economy. The declining trend in labor productivity in recent years poses an important challenge for the Singapore economy. As the knowledge-based economy takes stronger root in Singapore, the development of local human capital is crucial to sustain economic growth. Given the small pool of local human capital, the economy still relies on foreign manpower to leverage its competitiveness. However, the key policy stance is to develop local human capital and concurrently leverage foreign human capital to improve the innovative capabilities of the domestic industry.

5. IMPACT OF FOREIGN WORKERS ON PRODUCTIVITY AND WAGES IN THE MANUFACTURING SECTOR

What are the impacts of foreign workers on export competitiveness and capital investment in the manufacturing sector? In this section, we explore

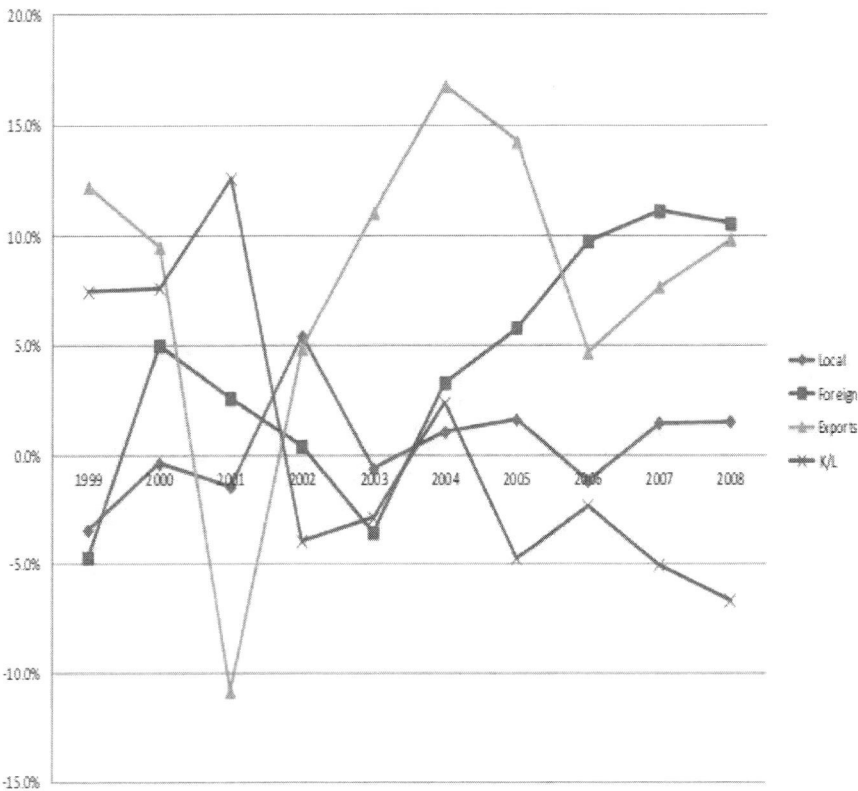

Figure 9. Growth Rate of Local Workers, Foreign Workers, Exports and Capital Intensity (Capital–Labor Ratio) in Manufacturing From 1998–2008.

Source: Report on Annual Census of Manufacturing Activities, EDB, various years.

the productive contribution of local and foreign workers in the manufacturing sector using the manufacturing industrial level from 1998 to 2008.

Figure 9 provides the key trends of exports, capital–labor rate, and local and foreign labor in the manufacturing sector. First, the local labor only grew around 1.4% in 1998–2008. Further, there seems to be some positive correlation between the growth rate of export and inflow of foreign workers. It is clear that the external shock from 9/11 terrorist attack has a strong negative impact on the exports of the manufacturing sector. Given that nearly 38% of manufactured export is destined for the

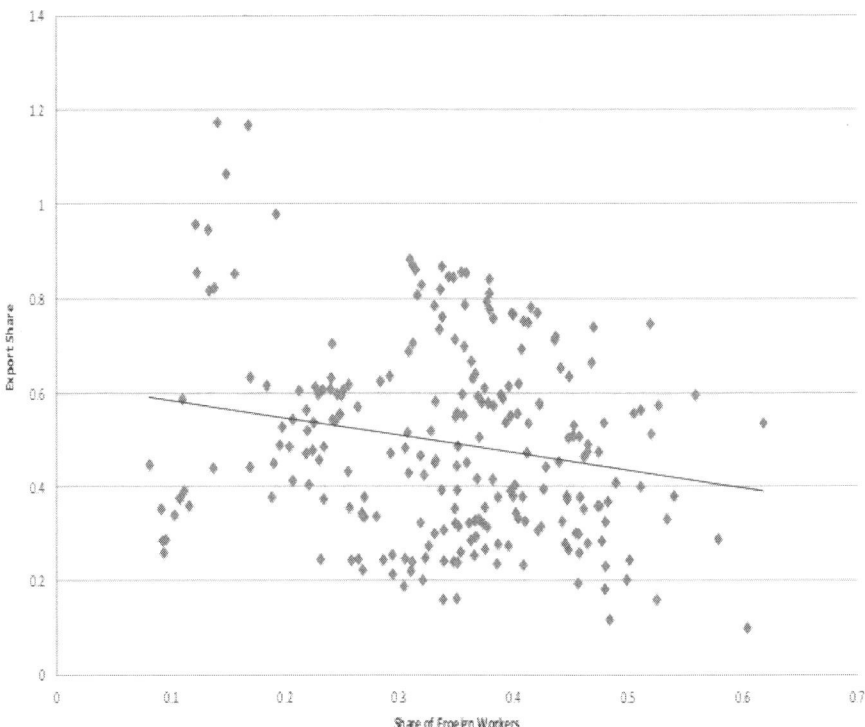

Figure 10. Export Share to Foreign Workers in Manufacturing From 1998–2008.
Source: Report on Annual Census of Manufacturing Activities, EDB, various years.

US and Europe, the Singapore economy went into a recession in 2001. Since 2002, there is some evidence that export might be in an upward trend.

Although we observe some positive trend between export and share of foreign workers at the aggregate level (see Fig. 9), the scatter plot by industries indicates otherwise. The scatter plot of export share to output and share of foreign workers, by industries, is given in Fig. 10. We observe a negative relationship between share of foreign workers and export share, indicating that industries with larger share of foreign workers tend to be less export-oriented. This suggests that larger flow of foreign workers might have some impact on the export competitiveness of the manufacturing sector.

94 *Inequality in Singapore*

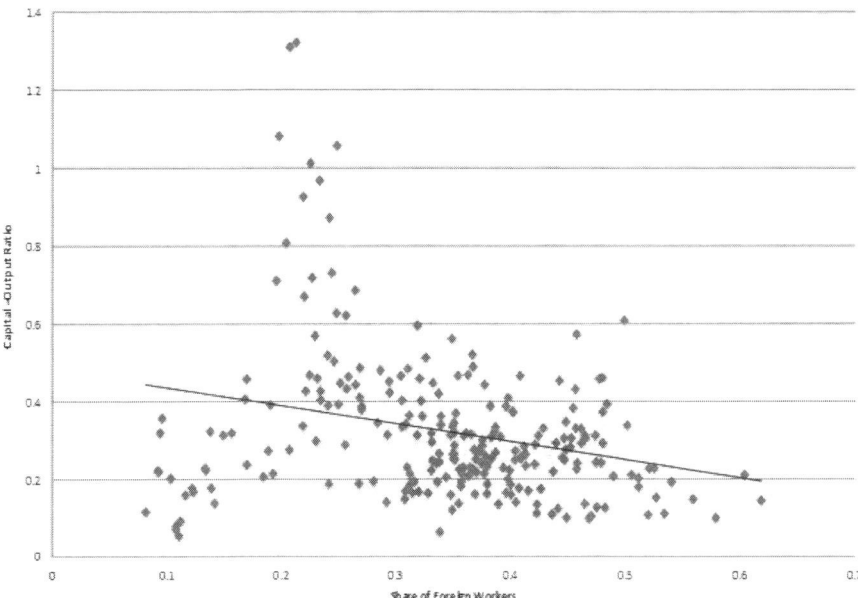

Figure 11. Capital–Output Ratio and Share of Foreign Workers in Manufacturing From 1998–2008.
Source: Report on Annual Census of Manufacturing Activities, EDB, various years.

The earlier Fig. 9 also reveals an interesting observation in terms of downward trend of capital–labor ratio since 1998 and negative growth since 2002. The scatter plot of capital to output ratio by industries, given in Fig. 11, reveals a negative relationship between inflow of foreign workers and capital investment decisions of firms. This suggests that most of the output growth in the manufacturing sector is driven by labor growth. This also indicates that the inflow of foreign workers and type of foreign workers tend to affect the capital investments and technology adoption of firms. With more open economy, firms tend to use cheaper and less skilled foreign workers thereby increasing their incentive to use existing or labor-intensive technologies as opposed to adopting new technologies through capital investments. The declining capital–labor ratio is of significant concern for the manufacturing sector, as this will have direct impact on the competitiveness of the manufacturing in the export market. Since new technologies are embodied in new capital investment, the declining

Table 3. Foreign Workers, Export, Capital–Labor Ratio, Local Wage Rate (Monthly) and Foreign Wage Rate (Monthly) for the Manufacturing Sector From 1998–2008.

	Share of foreign workers	Export share to output	Capital/labor ratio	Wage rate local ($)	Wage rate foreign ($)
1998–2002	0.384	0.602	123.22	3512.42	1993.27
2003–2008	0.415	0.613	123.77	4189.35	1994.54
2006–2008	0.446	0.610	117.17	4507.95	1997.63

capital–labor ratio indicates that workers might be producing output with less technology-intensive capital. The decision to adopt technology might also be affected by the large inflow of unskilled workers increasing the incentive to retain more labor-intensive technology. This is a major concern for the sustained growth of the Singapore economy.

Table 3 summarizes the trends of the key variables and provides some insights on the key trends of the wage rate of local and foreign workers. It is clear that the wage rate for the local workers is much higher than that of the foreign workers. In fact, the local wage rate is twice the foreign wage rate; it also increased by 19% in 2003–2008 as compared to 1998–2002, even with large inflow of foreign labor. It is clear that there is a positive growth trend in the wage rate of local workers, although there is a strong upward trend in the inflow of foreign workers. This indicates that there might be some complementarity between local and foreign workers in the manufacturing sector. This observation is also in line with the results of Chia *et al.* (2004).

6. THREE-SECTOR GENERAL EQUILIBRIUM MODEL FOR SINGAPORE

We further our study by simulating the impact of declining capital investments with greater inflow of foreign workers on the overall growth of the Singapore economy using a general equilibrium model. Several recent studies have attempted to measure the overall immigration surplus to the domestic economy using a partial and a general equilibrium framework (Borjas, 2003; Drinkwater *et al.*, 2007; Thangavelu, 2011). A recent study by Thangavelu (2011) on immigration surplus using a general equilibrium framework for the Singapore economy highlights the importance of highly skilled immigrants and investment in innovative activities affecting the overall immigration surplus in the domestic economy. Here, we just highlight the key results of the simulation and the model and the key parameters are available in Thangavelu (2011).

Thangavelu (2011) adopted the three-sector general equilibrium model with endogenous growth by Drinkwater *et al.* (2007) and calibrated it to the Singapore economy. Thangavelu's paper models three major sectors in the Singapore economy: a labor-intensive service sector, which is assumed to produce a homogeneous good where the value-add goes to physical capital accumulation; a capital-intensive manufacturing sector, which produces differentiated goods with growing varieties; and an innovative sector, which is assumed to be the economic engine of growth that conducts the necessary research activities for new product development. All sectors employ three factor inputs; namely, skilled workers, unskilled workers and physical capital. Since there is no closed-form solution, the paper adopted a numerical method, which narrowed the scope to the steady-state analysis. The full details of the three-sector general equilibrium model and the numerical solution for the steady-state values for the Singapore economy are given in Thangavelu (2011).

In the simulation with large unskilled workers and a weak innovation sector (or weak capital investments), the economy moderated to a steady-state growth of around 1.1% with a higher share of skilled foreign workers. With the share of total unskilled workers in the economy at nearly 45% of total employment, a higher share of unskilled foreign workers tends to lower steady-state growth. The simulation results of the steady-state growth rate with increasing inflow of skilled immigrants (or decrease in the share of unskilled foreign workers) for the scenario of higher share of unskilled workers are shown in Fig. 12.

From Fig. 12, there is clear evidence that there is a positive effect of the skilled immigrants on the steady-state growth rate of around 1.1%, and it also increases the size of the innovative sector when their fraction within the total immigrant workforce is increased. The inflow of skilled immigrants relative to unskilled workers tends to encourage more research activities in the economy and hence promote long-term growth. However,

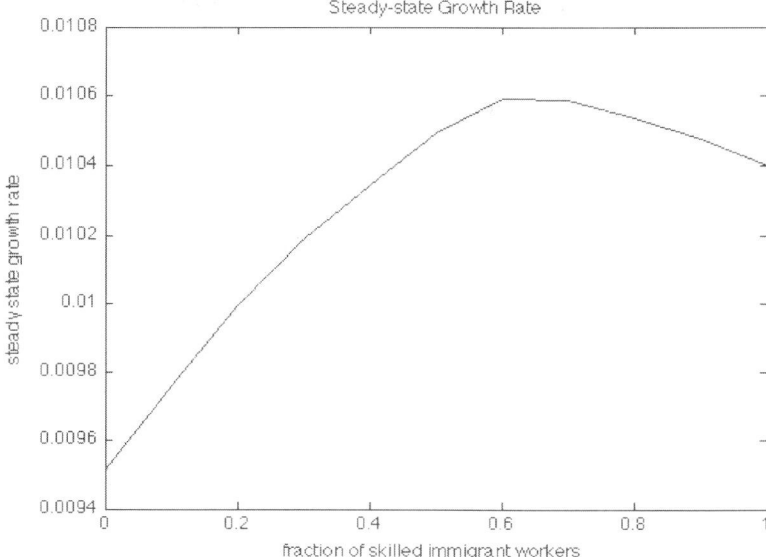

Figure 12. Steady-State Growth Rate With Low Technological Innovation.
Source: Author's calculations.

the increase in skilled immigrants in the economy tends to increase the growth rate and size of the research and development sector at a diminishing rate (due to weak capital investments), and both variables started to decline when the fraction of the skilled immigrants exceeded a threshold of 60%. The diminishing return is expected to set in once the reward from the complementarities between the physical capital and the skilled immigrants are fully exploited. The "crowding-out" effect on the total physical capital causes the steady-state growth rate and the size of the innovative sector to decrease after reaching the threshold. The maximum percentage growth gain is achieved when the physical capital is fully exploited by the skilled workers in the economy, which corresponds to a 60% of the skilled workers among immigrants.

In the second simulation (see Fig. 13), the flow of total foreign workers was moderated by maintaining the share of foreign at 30% of the total labor force. The skilled employment share in the pre-immigration state is also taken to be higher at 0.55 and 0.45 for unskilled workers. This reflects

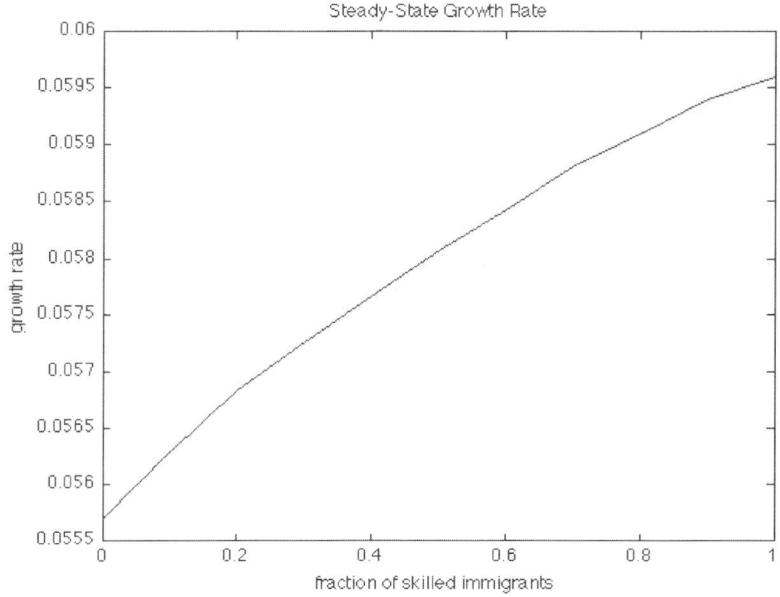

Figure 13. Steady-State Growth Rate With High Technological Innovation.
Source: Author's calculations.

the current government policy to increase the number of skilled workers in the economy and concurrently moderate the flow of unskilled foreign workers.

It is interesting to observe that the high share of skilled workers produces a higher steady-state growth rate of nearly 5% and the economy also experience less diminishing returns due to the increasing share of skilled immigrants on the output growth and conversely on the innovative sector (see Fig. 13). This result is mainly driven by the high share of capital accumulation (or capital share) in the innovative sector, and thus there is a greater complementarity between skilled and capital investments which is not fully exploited. The greater inflow of skilled immigrants tends to complement capital and increase the innovative activities in the domestic economy, thus leading to higher steady-state growth.

The simulation result of the wage gap is reflected in Fig. 14. It is interesting to observe that the wage gap between the skilled and unskilled narrows as the foreign share is maintained at 40% of the workforce. This is

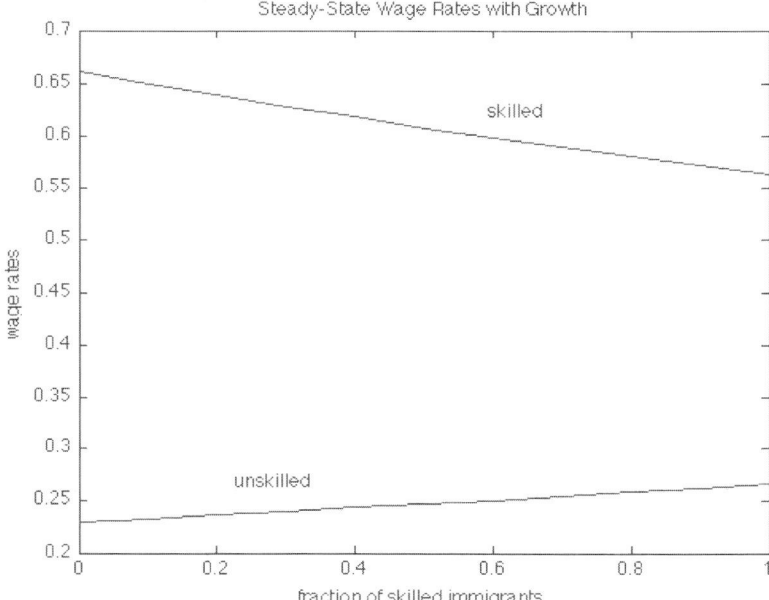

Figure 14. Steady-State Wage Gap With High Technology Innovation.
Source: Author's calculations.

mainly due to the increased supply of skilled workers in the economy due to the inflow of skilled immigrants and the reduction of unskilled foreign workers in the economy. We also observe that the factor share of unskilled workers also increases moderately as their demand rises due to higher output growth.

7. POLICY CONCLUSIONS

The paper studies the impact of immigrants on the Singapore economy. The results clearly indicate that the Singapore economy is relying on foreign labor to augment domestic human capital and complement the declining domestic labor force due to aging and falling fertility rate.

However, the rising flow of foreign labor also has several effects on the domestic economy. The results clearly indicate that although foreign workers make productive contribution, it is much lower as compared to local workers. The analysis of the paper indicates that inflow of foreign labor has little impact on the wage rate of local workers. In fact, we do observe rising wage rate for local workers in periods of high inflow of foreign labor. This suggests that foreign labor is likely to complement local labor. However, the complementary effects between local and foreign workers are likely to be at different skill levels. A study by Ottaviano and Peri (2008) examined the complementary and substitution effects between local and foreign workers in the US economy. The data on different skill types of local and foreign workers are not available for the Singapore economy and this could be possible extensions of the current study.

The declining capital–labor ratio in the manufacturing sector is of great concern to the Singapore economy. The declining capital–labor ratio is also in line with high inflow of foreign labor, thereby suggesting that large inflow of foreign workers might affect the investment decisions of firms to adopt new technologies. As indicated by Peri (2009), large inflow of foreign workers is likely to increase the low skill-biased technology investment as observed in the US economy. The results of the paper indicate that the productivity of foreign workers increases with less capital investment, thereby indicating that foreign workers are more productive with less capital and technology-intensive production structure. In contrast, local workers are more productive with high capital investment, indicating that there is more complementarity between capital investments and local human capital. Thus the skill types of foreign workers do affect the technology adoption decisions of firms and hence their competitiveness.

We also observed that the Singapore economy is experiencing decreasing returns to scale in the manufacturing sector. This might be due to the declining capital investment and hence lack of investment in new technology and capital. The results of the study indicate that with declining investment in technology, together with increasing reliance on foreign workers in the past decade, manufacturing firms might be operating with technologies and organization structures that are not competitive. In particular, we also observed that decreasing returns to scale has greater impact on the productivity of local workers as compared to foreign workers who are more transient in the domestic labor market. This indicates a strong relationship between capital investment in new technologies and domestic human capital accumulation for the manufacturing sector. This has important implications for the competitiveness of the Singapore manufacturing sector and export growth in the long run. However, given the lack of skilled and unskilled labor data, we are not able to explore this important issue between human capital and fixed capital investment in the manufacturing sector.

There are several key implications from foreign workers in terms of balancing innovation and growth in the domestic economy. The result of the model simulation indicates that skilled immigrants do exert a positive effect on the indigenous economy, but at a diminishing rate. Skilled immigrants tend to encourage more research activities in the economy and hence promote long-term growth. We also observed that diminishing returns begin when the reward from the complementarity effect between physical capital and skilled immigrants is fully exploited.

The simulation results also highlight that moderating foreign workers at 40% of the workforce with high capital intensity produces positive output growth. In this equilibrium, we also observe higher steady-state growth with a higher share of skilled foreign workers. The rising share of skilled foreign workers reduces the skilled wage rate and also the wage gap between skilled and unskilled workers in the economy.

The results also indicate that the positive impact of immigrants, and in particular skilled immigrants, depend on innovative activities in the economy. In particular, there is diminishing return from having additional skilled foreign workers in the economy, for a given level of capital stock in the economy. This indicates that there is a threshold level of skilled immigrants that will have a positive impact on the innovative sector and growth of the economy. This is crucial for Asian economies to drive their innovation activities. This is particularly important for the Singapore economy as it moderates the flow of foreign workers and increases its competitiveness in the global economy.

Investments in local human capital are also vital for the long-term growth of Singapore's economy. In a globalized environment, workers have to constantly upgrade their skills to stay relevant. At present, most training programs are designed for and targeted at low-skilled local workers. This enables them to improve their productivity levels and command higher wages, thereby reducing wage inequality. With the shift toward higher value-added activities, Singapore will need to implement general training schemes for the entire workforce and also make human capital portable across industries. Constant re-training and skills upgrading is necessary to meet the rapidly evolving demands of the labor market. These investments in local human capital will grant productivity gains, thereby improving the long-term growth potential of the Singapore economy.

This study could be extended in several directions. Firstly, the results indicate that skilled types might have some impact on the technology adoption and productive performance of the economy. However, we do not have the data by skill types of local and foreign workers to study impact of skilled types on productive performance of workers.

Further, we are also not able to empirically study the impact of foreign workers on wages of local workers in the economy due to the lack of detail data by skill types. A study by Borjas (2003) on the US economy indicates that native wages decline with inflow of foreign immigrants, and the greatest decline is for workers with low skills. However, the study by Ottaviano and Peri (2008) using a general equilibrium approach shows a positive impact of immigrants on native wages in the US economy. A positive effect of immigration on native wages was also found in separate studies by Card (2004) and Peri (2007), despite a large proportion of low-skilled workers examined amongst the migrant populations. Thus it might be interesting to examine the impact of foreign workers on the native wages using more micro-level data and general equilibrium framework.

It might also be important to study the welfare implications of foreign workers in terms of economic and social welfare for the domestic economy. The inflow of foreign workers not only creates economic effects on the domestic economy — there are several social implications of having a large inflow of foreign workers in the economy in terms of competing for public infrastructure and affecting the local cultural diversity in the economy. The overall net social benefit to the economy seems to be related to the assimilation of foreign workers to the domestic economy and myriad cultures (Chiswick, 1978; LaLonde and Topel, 1992; Borjas, 2003).

The results of the paper supports the recent policy recommendations of the Economic Strategic Committee (ESC) in terms of increasing the medium- to long-term growth of the Singapore economy by increasing productivity growth and reducing the reliance on foreign workers. For a small and open economy, policies on capital and labor mobility will be crucial to sustain the competitiveness of the economy. The Singapore economy has effectively managed to balance capital and labor mobility to enhance the overall competitiveness of the economy since its independence. As the domestic economy moves toward a knowledge-based one, the impact of foreign capital and labor on the innovative activities of the small and open economy will be crucial. Even with the large inflow of skilled workers, Thangavelu (2011) indicates that the positive impact of immigrants and, in particular skilled immigrants, depends on innovative activities in the economy. In particular, there is diminishing return from having additional skilled foreign workers in the economy, for a given level of capital stock in the economy. This indicates that there is a threshold level of skilled immigrants that will have a positive impact on the innovative sector and growth of the economy. This is crucial as Singapore moderates its flow of foreign workers and increases its competitiveness in the global economy.

APPENDIX A

By definition,

$$\text{GDP} = [\text{GDP}/L] * L \tag{A.1}$$

Taking logarithm of variables on both side of Eq. (1):

$$\log \text{GDP} = \log (\text{GDP}/L) + \log L$$
$$= \log (\text{GDP}/L) + \log [LW + FW] \tag{A.2}$$

In Eq. (2), total employment (L) is partitioned into local employed workers (LW) and foreign employed workers (FW).

Differentiating the Eq. (2) with respect to time:

$$\partial \log \text{GDP}/\partial t = \partial \log (\text{GDP}/L)/\partial t$$
$$+ (LW/L)\partial LW/\partial t + (FW/L)\partial FW/\partial t; \tag{A.3}$$

which is decomposed as:

Growth of GDP = growth of productivity
  + share of local workers * growth of local workers
  + share of foreign workers * growth in foreign workers. (A.4)

(See *Chia et al.*, 2004)

APPENDIX B

TYPES OF FOREIGN WORKERS IN SINGAPORE

B.1. EP

a. EP Holders: The EP is targeted at skilled foreign workers employed as professionals and executives in Singapore. The eligibility criteria for EP is that skilled foreign worker (a) earn a fixed monthly salary of more than $2500 and (b) have a recognized qualification (see Ministry of Manpower website).
b. There are three categories of EP:
   1. P1 pass is for foreign workers earning a fixed monthly salary of more than $7000.
   2. P2 pass is for foreign workers earning a fixed monthly salary between $3500 and $7000 and possesses recognized qualifications.
   3. Q1 pass is for foreign workers earning a fixed monthly salary between $2500 and $3500 and possesses recognized qualifications.

B.2. SP

a. SP applies to mid-level skilled workers such as technicians and semi-skilled workers applying for professional and specialized jobs.
b. SP applicants are assessed in terms of point system that includes salary, educational qualifications, skills, job type and experience.
c. Foreign workers are eligible to apply for SP if they earn a monthly salary of at least $1800 and possesses recognized qualifications with a minimum level of a degree or diploma.
d. The employment of SP is subject to a quota (dependency ceiling) of 25% of the company's total workforce.

B.3. WP

a. WP applies to foreign workers earning a monthly basic salary of not more than $1800.
b. The prospective employer must first apply to Ministry of Manpower for a WP before employing a foreign worker (minimum age of 16 years).

c. Skilled WP applies to foreign workers with at least a recognized national trade certificate [NTC-3 (Practical) Trade Certificate] or equivalent that is relevant to the worker's occupation.
d. Employer pays a lower levy for skilled WP foreign workers.

[Information as on 2011]

8. COMMENTS ON PRESENTATION BY SPEAKER

Discussant: Ms Wong Su-Yen

Senior Partner and ASEAN Managing Director, Mercer

Research Contributor: Ms Tan Wei-Lin

Senior Associate, Mercer

Earlier in 2012, Mercer collaborated with the World Economic Forum (WEF) to release a comprehensive report on *Talent Mobility Good Practices — Collaboration at the Core of Driving Economic Growth*.[3] The global report highlights that the most effective way to address labor market failures and enhance job creation is for stakeholders on all sides of the employment equation to work together toward improving talent mobility — and move jobs to people and people to jobs. This could involve moving people across business units and job families, across organizations, within industries and regions, and across occupations and skillsets. It could also include moving jobs to people through external labor market analysis and site selection.

There is a serious imbalance in the world's human capital markets today. In most of Asia, we see abundant opportunities but a lack of talent to support growth; in the West and in more developed economies, there is a mismatch of available skills against what is demanded by companies, with high unemployment and employability challenges slowing down economies and threatening future growth globally. The magnitude and risk of this imbalance is dire and requires concrete action and collaboration by governments, businesses and educational institutions across the world.

---

[3] To download the full report, please go to: http://www.mercer.com/globaltalent.

In addressing Singapore's need to manage foreign labor and local human capital in its quest to achieve balanced growth, we can draw insights from this report which highlights talent mobility as an enabler for private companies, governments, academic institutions and NGOs to close skill gaps and remedy talent shortages, while also moving more people to employability and employment. In response to particular labor market failures, talent mobility practices can effectively boost labor supply, stimulate labor demand, or better equilibrate supply and demand through changes in the cost or quantity of labor — all of which lead to growth.

In fact, findings from the report show that while there are many examples of good practices that can be adopted to help rebalance global talent markets, talent mobility is not achieving its full potential. The report points out that talent markets are impeded by four key problems: widespread unemployability, skill gaps, information gaps and private and public constraints on mobility. These issues are pervasive and daunting with many countries and regions struggling with high unemployment and untapped labor pools, while many industry sectors and employers face talent shortages and skill gaps.

With unemployment rate at a mere 2%, Singapore's challenge lies predominantly in finding enough skilled talent to fuel economic growth — albeit through the carefully balanced deployment of local and foreign talent. Drawing from ideas presented in the same report, talent mobility practices that can help address these challenges include:

8.1. Addressing Unemployability

Basic employment training and employment subsidies can help reduce the unemployability of some Singaporeans, which exists because of the lack of basic employment skills, particularly among people in underprivileged communities or older age groups. This has negative consequences for individuals who are shut out of the labor market, for societies deprived of economic opportunity, and for businesses that need skilled people to drive growth.

Organizations and governments in Singapore need to continue working together to train and educate those lacking the relevant skills for employment to increase labor market participation, through for example, training initiatives and subsidies offered by Singapore's Workforce Development Agency (WDA).

8.2. Addressing Skill Gaps

Retraining and up-skilling the workforce as well as enhanced focus on career development can help close skill gaps. Critical skill gaps exist between what employees possess and what businesses need. Because of these gaps, businesses cannot find the talent they need where they need it and individuals may find themselves ill-equipped for the jobs of the future. The world is changing everyday with transformations in technology, consumer habits, social norms and values. Employers, government agencies, and individuals each play an essential role in ensuring skills, too, evolve and keep up with the times.

8.3. Addressing Information Gaps

Workers lack information about current job openings or future skill needs, while employers seeking talent cannot perfectly observe the actual capabilities of prospective employees. Potential solutions include increasing the information available to individuals and employers, improving workforce planning within organizations, strengthening and credentialing to fill information gaps. Information gaps make it difficult for labor markets to match workers to jobs effectively. Workforce communication systems within organizations are key in this regard, as are government platforms, industry associations, and business chambers that facilitate networks and flow of information across the entire labor market. Improving the signaling power of credentials also help job seekers and employers find each other.

8.4. Easing Constraints on Talent Mobility

This involves easing migration and facilitating mobility within organizations, and moving jobs to people to reduce constraints on mobility. Public and private constraints on mobility impede the ability of markets to balance supply and demand by adjusting wages or the number of workers. These include common government interventions, such as imposing minimum wage laws and visa restrictions; and private ones, such as imposing union rules or professional credentialing restrictions.

In Singapore, the government faces an important and difficult challenge, which is to ensure adequate and appropriate human capital to drive future growth, balanced against backlash from citizens who have perceived labor policies to be overly pro-foreigner. The issues at hand are complex and go beyond jobs and wages. The government needs to carefully manage its foreign and local talent in a way that maintains the social fabric and societal harmony while enabling continued economic growth.

In summary, when multiple stakeholders across the public and private sectors collaborate, they can design policies that simultaneously address unemployability, skill gaps, information gaps and mobility constraints. Collaboration among multiple stakeholders is at the core of successful talent mobility practices. Whether on the organizational level, within an industry, within Singapore alone or across Asia, or across multiple stakeholders worldwide, collaboration with the right mindset in place enables stakeholders to grapple effectively with talent market challenges to significantly enhance growth.

REFERENCES

Arellano, M and S Bond (1991). Some tests of specification for panel data: Monte Carlo evidence and an application to employment equations. *Review of Economic Studies*, 58, 277–297.

Blundell, R and S Bond. (1998). Initial conditions and moment restrictions in dynamic panel data models. *Journal of Econometrics*, 87(1), 115–143.

Blundell, RW and SR Bond (2000). GMM estimation with persistent panel data: an application to production function. *Econometric Reviews*, 19(3), 321–340.

Blundell, RW, SR Bond and F Windmeijer (2000). Estimation in dynamic panel data models: improving on the performance of standard GMM estimators. Working paper series no. 00/12, Institute for Fiscal Studies, London.

Bond, S, A Hoeffler and J Temple (2001). GMM estimation of empirical growth models. Economic papers 2001-W21, University of Oxford, Nuffield College, Economics group.

Borjas, GJ (1999). The economic analysis of immigration. In *Handbook of Labor Economics Vol. 3A*, O Ashenfelter and D Card (eds.), pp. 1697–1760. Amsterdam: Elsevier.

Borjas, GJ (2003). The labor demand curve is downward sloping: re-examining the impact of immigration on the labor market. *Quarterly Journal of Economics*, 118(4), 1335–1374.

Borjas, GJ (2009). The analytics of the wage effect of immigration. NBER working paper no. 14796, National Bureau of Economic Research, Cambridge.

Borjas, GJ, RB Freeman and LF Katz (1996). Searching for the effect of immigration on the labor market. *American Economic Review*, 86(2), 246–251.

Borjas, GJ, J Grogger and G Hanson (2008). Imperfect substitutes between immigrants and natives: a reappraisal. NBER working paper no.13887, National Bureau of Economic Research, Cambridge.

Card, DE (2004). Is the new immigration really so bad? CReAM discussion paper series CDP No. 0402, Centre for Research and Analysis of Migration, University College London, Department of Economics.

Chander, P and SM Thangavelu (2005). Technology adoption, education and immigration policies. *Journal of Development Economics*, 75, 79–94.

Chia, B, SM Thangavelu and MH Toh (2004). The complimentary role of foreign in Singapore. *Economic Survey of Singapore, First Quarter 2004*. Singapore: MTI.

Chiswick, BR (1978). The effect of Americanization on the earnings of foreign born men. *Journal of Political Economy*, 86(5), 897–921.

Chang, HC (2002). Do foreign workers have an adverse effect on the native unskilled labor in Taiwan? Working papers series 859, University of Melbourne, Department of Economics.

Choi, YY (2004). The macroeconomic impact of foreign labor influx into the industrialized nation state and the complementary policies. *Applied Economics*, 36, 1057–1063.

Drinkwater, S, P Levine, E Lottie and J Pearlman (2007). The immigration surplus revised in a general equilibrium model with endogenous growth. *Journal of Regional Science*, 47(3), 569–601.

Hui, WT and AR Hashmi (2007). Foreign labor and economic growth policy options for Singapore. *The Singapore Economic Review (SER)*, 52(01), 53–72.

Hunt, J and M Gauthier-Loiselle (2008). How much does immigration boost innovation? NBER working paper no. 14312, National Bureau of Economic Research, Cambridge.

Kangasniemi, M, M Mas, C Robinson and L Serrano (2008). The economic impact of migration — productivity analysis for Spain and the UK. MPRA paper 15835, University Library of Munich, Germany.

LaLonde, RJ and RH Topel (1992). The assimilation of immigrants in the US labor market. In *Immigration and the Work Force: Economic Consequences for the United States and Source Areas*, GJ Borjas and RB Freeman (eds.), pp. 67–92. Chicago: University of Chicago Press.

Levine, P, E Lotti and J Pearlman (2003). The immigration surplus revisited in a general equilibrium model with endogenous growth. Discussion paper no. 0203, University of Surrey, Department of Economics.

Ministry of Manpower, Singapore (2004). Employment trend and structure. MRSD working paper no. 2/2004.

Ministry of Manpower, Singapore (2008a). Employment of Singapore citizens, permanent residents, and foreigners: 1997–2006. MRSD paper no. 1/2008.

Ministry of Manpower, Singapore (2008b). Manpower 2008. MRSD.

Ministry of Manpower, Singapore (2009). Manpower 2009. MRSD.

Mountford, A (1999). Can a brain drain be good for growth in the source economy? *Journal of Development Economics*, 53(2), 287–303.

Orrenius, PM and M Zavodny (2007). Does immigration affect wages? A look at occupation-level evidence. *Labor Economics*, 14(5), 757–773.

Ottaviano, GP and G Peri (2008). Rethinking the effect of immigration on wages. NBER working paper no. 12497, National Bureau of Economic Research, Cambridge.

Peri, G (2007). Immigrants' complementarities and native wages: evidence from California. NBER working paper no. 12956, National Bureau of Economic Research, Cambridge.

Peri, G (2009). The effect of immigration on productivity: evidence from US states. NBER working paper no. 15507, National Bureau of Economic Research, Cambridge.

Peri, G and C Sparber (2009). Task specialization, immigration, and wages. *American Economic Journal: Applied Economics*, 1(3), 135–169.

Stark, O and Y Wang (2002). Inducing human capital formation: migration as a substitute for subsidies. *Journal of Public Economics*, 86(1), 29–46.

Tan, KY, F Wu, MH Toh and KW Seah (2001). Has foreign labor contributed to Singapore's economic growth: an empirical assessment. *Economic Survey of Singapore, Third Quarter 2001*. Singapore: MTI.

Thangavelu, SM (2011). Immigration surplus, innovation, and wage gap: dynamic competitive general equilibrium model of Singapore with immigration. National University of Singapore, Department of Economics.

Vidal, JP (1998). The effect of emigration on human capital formation. *Journal of Population Economics*, 11(4), 589–600.

CHAPTER 6

HEALTH CARE AND LONG-TERM CARE

Health and Long-term Care for the Aging Population in Singapore

SPEAKER: ASSOCIATE PROFESSOR PHUA KAI HONG
Lee Kuan Yew School of Public Policy,
National University of Singapore

RESEARCH CONTRIBUTORS: MS TANIA NG
Lee Kuan Yew School of Public Policy,
National University of Singapore

MR WINSTON CHIN
Saw Swee Hock School of Public Health,
National University of Singapore

1. INTRODUCTION

Singapore, like many other developed countries in the world, is facing the challenge of an acutely aging population, driven by rising life expectancies and declining fertility rates. The proportion of the resident population aged 65 years and over rose from 3.4% in 1970 to 9.9% in 2012 (Singapore Department of Statistics, 2012), and is projected to reach 18.7% by 2030 (Singapore Committee on Ageing Issues, 2013). The old-age support ratio, i.e., persons aged 20–64 years per elderly aged 65 years and over, dropped from 13.5 in 1970 to 6.7 in 2012. Life expectancy has increased dramatically, from 65.8 years in 1970 to 82.0 years in 2011.

The elderly population has unique health needs, including a high prevalence of chronic diseases like diabetes, heart disease and stroke, functional disability, and diseases causing cognitive impairment such as dementia. A study in 2005 found that 6.6% of those aged 65 years or older had disability in at least one of five ADL (activities of daily living) items, higher than previous reported prevalence in Singapore (Ng *et al.*, 2006). It has been projected that the prevalence rate of dementia in Singapore will rise to 1.75% in 2030 from 0.65% in 2010, translating to 92,000 elderly persons living with dementia (Access Economics, 2006).

The specific health issues of the elderly have necessitated a worldwide paradigm shift away from episodic hospital-centric care, toward long-term care. While the definition of "long-term care" (LTC) is debatable, it generally entails a range of services that aims to support the elderly with functional and cognitive disability, either in the community or in residential facilities like nursing homes. In recent decades, much attention has been given to long-term care policy, especially the aspects of service organization, delivery and financing. Faced with economic uncertainty and spiralling government budgetary deficits, many Western developed countries have also been forced to reconsider their approaches to health care financing to achieve greater fiscal sustainability.

2. HEALTH AND SOCIAL CARE POLICY FOR POPULATION AGING IN SINGAPORE

The Singapore government's philosophy on care of the elderly is that the family should be the first line of support. Elderly who are frail or ill should be cared for by family at home as far as possible, with institutionalization as a last resort. Community services should support the family in this caregiving role. In addition, older Singaporeans should assume personal responsibility for their health, particularly in living healthy lifestyles and ensuring their continued employability and financial security (Singapore Inter-Ministerial Committee on Ageing, 1999).

For the provision of long-term care for the elderly, the government's strategy is for non-governmental voluntary welfare organizations (VWOs) to be service providers, while the government plays the role of direction-setting, financing and regulation. The government does not provide any services directly, the rationale being that (1) anything provided by the government is considered a "right", which leads to increased demand, and (2) such services often require a level of motivation and compassion, and VWOs can also garner voluntary support (Ling, 1998). This trend of partnership between government and charitable organizations in the provision of long-term care services is also seen in many other countries.

Health services for the elderly can be seen in terms of part of a "care continuum", of which long-term care is only one part. Figure 1 illustrates the various components of this care continuum, and examples of different facilities catering to specific needs in Singapore.

Currently, all long-term care services are provided by VWOs, with some for-profit providers. The government provides various kinds of assistance to these VWOs (see Table 1).

To promote integration and continuity of care between different providers, the Ministry of Health (MOH) set up a statutory board called the Agency for Integrated Care (AIC). AIC assesses individual patients and refers them to appropriate providers, and helps acute hospitals co-ordinate patient discharges to appropriate step-down facilities like community hospitals and nursing homes.

The government recently announced a raft of new measures to boost the capacity of the long-term care sector, including increasing nursing

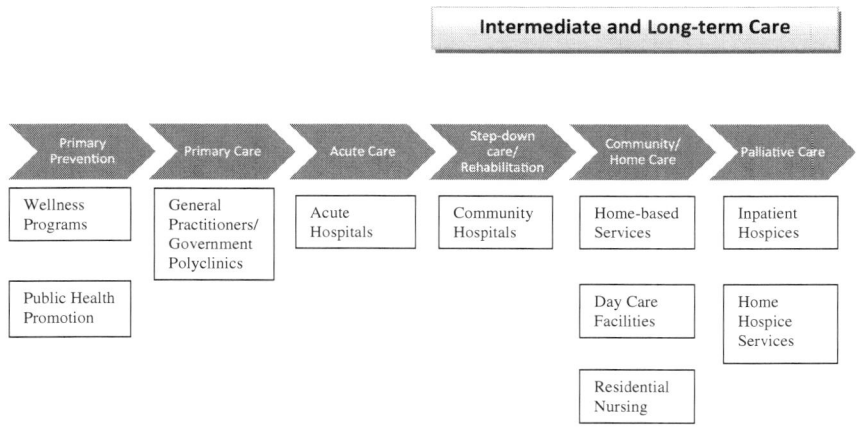

Figure 1. The Continuum of Care for Elderly.

Table 1. Government Assistance to VWOs in the Provision of the Intermediate and Long-term Care (ILTC) Services.

Financial Assistance	Up to 90% for capital expenditure
	Up to 90% for cyclical maintenance costs for existing building
	Up to 50% for operating/recurrent expenditure
	Up to 100% rental subsidy for use of government premises or state land
	100% rebate for input Goods and Services Tax (GST)
Manpower Assistance	Secondment of doctors and nurses to work in VWO facilities
	Facilitating the allocation of foreign workers permits, and waiving the foreign workers' levy for VWOs
	Training of nursing aides
Others	Facilitate the allocation of state land and premises
	Exemption for Certificate of Entitlement (COE) for vehicles used in providing services run by the VWOs
	Issue medical fee exemption cards to needy residents requiring residential care
	Provision of guidelines on nursing home standards and care requirements

home bed capacity by 70%, increasing home-based health care and social services capacity, and increasing day social and rehabilitative care places (Singapore Ministerial Committee on Ageing, 2012). In addition, it has also announced additional funding to VWO nursing homes to improve staffing ratios, dedicated funds to enable pay increases in the ILTC sector, and investment in initiatives to improve productivity, quality and professional development (Singapore Ministry of Health, 2012a, 2012c). The Community Silver Trust (CST) is a dollar-for-dollar donation-matching grant provided by the government to VWOs in the intermediate and long-term care sectors.

To better support informal caregivers of elderly in the community, it is also working with VWOs and other training providers to develop more caregiver training courses, and has launched a new $120 Foreign Domestic Worker Grant (FDWG) for families with a per capita income of up to $2200, who require the assistance of a foreign domestic worker to care for elderly patients with severe dementia (Singapore Ministry of Community, Youth and Sports, 2012).

3. HEALTH AND LONG-TERM CARE FINANCING IN SINGAPORE

For financing of long-term care, the government has continued its twin philosophy of shared responsibility, targeting government support for lower-income groups through means-testing. The fundamental "3M" system that underlies the medical care system (Medisave, MediShield and Medifund) has been reviewed elsewhere (Phua, 2002; Lim, 2004). Payment for long-term care services, as in the rest of the health care system, functions on a co-payment basis. Subsidies for long-term care services are provided on a means-tested basis, depending on per capita household income per month. Under the latest revised subsidy framework announced in 2012, the qualifying per capita household monthly income was raised from $1400 to $2200 for home, community-based and residential long-term care services, covering two-thirds of all households. The degree of subsidy ranges from 20%, up to a maximum of 80% for those with per capita household income less than $600 (Singapore Ministry of Health, 2012b). Subsidies are only available to VWO providers; private providers are not eligible for subsidies, except for a small group of approved private nursing homes that enjoy portable government subsidies.

ElderShield, a severe disability insurance scheme, was introduced in 2002 to further help citizens meet expenses incurred in the event of severe disability. It is run by government-appointed private insurers on actuarial principles. Singapore citizens and Permanent Residents are automatically enrolled on an opt-out basis at age of 40, and pay premiums from their Medisave accounts annually until age 65. Severely disabled persons (defined as limitations in at least three out of six ADLs), receive a monthly cash payout of $300 or $400 for up to 60 or 72 months, respectively, (depending on the scheme (Singapore Ministry of Health, n.d.). For those who were not eligible to join ElderShield due to age or pre-existing disabilities, the government has instituted the Interim Disability Assistance Programme for the Elderly (IDAPE), which provides $100 or $150 month per month for a maximum of 72 months, with a qualifying per capita monthly household income ceiling of $1000. Higher IDAPE payouts were announced in 2012.

In light of increasing concerns about the affordability of health care in Singapore, the government has recently announced that it will be undertaking a comprehensive review of the health care financing system, including long-term care and the ElderShield scheme. It has also announced its intention to increase the share of government spending on health care, with more targeted support for specialist outpatient care, primary care, preventive health care and long-term care (Singapore Ministry of Health, 2013).

3.1. Singapore's Health care Financing System

Chief to understanding the health care financing system in Singapore is to examine the Community Provident Fund (CPF). Employers and employees contribute a percentage of an individual's wages to the person's private CPF account; and this can be withdrawn for an individual's retirement when the person turns 55, when the CPF Minimum Sum (MS) requirements are met. The monthly CPF contribution is then allocated in varying proportions into three accounts — Ordinary Account (OA), Special Account (SA) and Medisave.

Medisave forms the cornerstone of the health care financing system and is used to meet their personal or their dependants' health care expenses,[1] especially during retirement. Medisave can be used to pay for the hospitalization and certain outpatient expenses. Along with the Medisave, there is MediShield which covers hospitalization bills for treatment of catastrophic illnesses or prolonged hospitalizations at Class B2/C wards in restructured hospitals as well as certain approved outpatient treatments. For additional coverage that will allow for treatment in private hospitals or in Class A/B1 wards in restructured hospitals, individuals can purchase a Medisave-approved Integrated Shield Plan (IP). This is an enhancement plan offered by a private insurer and the premiums for an IP can be paid using Medisave.

Finally there is the Medical Endowment Fund (Medifund), which is an endowment set up by the Singapore government to help needy Singaporeans

---

[1] Dependents refer to spouse, children, parents and grandparents. Grandparents must be Singaporeans or Singapore Permanent Residents (SPRs).

to pay for their medical expenses despite the subsidized rates at restructured hospitals and the existence of Medisave and MediShield. Together, they form the "3Ms" of the Singapore health care financing system and have been a major means by which the Singapore government ensures majority of the population have access to good medical care (see Table 2 below).

The "3Ms" have effectively devolved the burden of health care financing onto the individual. Between 2006 and 2011, government expenditure on health care hovered between only 0.8% and 1.2% of gross domestic product (GDP). This means that 2–3 GDP percentage points of the national health care expenditure is made up of private expenditure. The amount of government expenditure on health care cuts an impressively low figure, but this begets the question about the ability of Singapore's health care system to ensure good health care delivery and outcomes. While the health care system has served the nation well in the past, cracks have surfaced in the system, given the demographic changes in the Singapore population.

The Singapore government has guaranteed universal coverage by ensuring that no Singaporean will be denied access to basic health care because of affordability issues. The existence of Medifund is one such financing mechanism to ensure that no Singaporeans fall through the gaps. The government is also cognizant that a growing elderly population is going to see more low-income elderly needing financial assistance. Aware that the intermediate to long-term nature of nursing care can be a

Table 2. Medisave, MediShield and Integrated Shield Plans Coverage.

	2007	2008	2009	2010	Revised 2011
Proportion of Class B2/C bills fully covered by Medisave withdrawal limits (%)	90	84	84	82	>80
Average proportion paid by MediShield for large Class B2/C bills (%)	52	62	62	62	>60
Average coverage of Class B2/C bills by Medisave withdrawal limits (%)	98	96	96	95	>90

Source: MOH, expenditure estimates from FY 2011 & FY 2012.

financial drain to many elderly individuals and family, the government established the Eldercare Fund in 2000. The fund is aimed at providing operating subsidies to nursing homes run by VWOs. This is achieved with the interest income earned from a capital injection of $2.5 billion into the endowment with public monies. The government, however, stresses that this is not to replace community donations and fund-raising efforts, but to supplement the community support infrastructure. In addition, a portion of Medifund was carved out in 2007 to establish Medifund Silver to deliver targeted financial aid to elderly Singaporeans aged 65 years and above. Medifund Silver can be tapped for bills incurred in restructured hospital as well as Medifund-approved institutions in the ILTC sectors.

The Singapore government has also long espoused the "family as the first line of support" as part of its "many helpings hands" approach in delivering social support. The current cohort of older persons is thus largely reliant on transfers from family, but this may not necessarily be the most definitive source of financial support. In the National Survey of Senior Citizens (NSSC) conducted in 1995, approximately 80% of older persons aged 65 years and above were dependent on their children for financial support. However, given the changing mores of the society and globalization, such network transfers appear to be in danger of breaking down. Survey results from the 2005 NSSC conducted indicated that approximately 60% of older persons aged 65 years and above were being financially supported by their children. The Singapore government sought to pre-empt the problem by passing the Maintenance of Parents Act (MPA) in 1996 to legislatively mandate adult children to provide for their elderly parents.

4. ADEQUACY OF CURRENT HEALTH CARE FINANCING

With the rising longevity of Singaporeans, this has led to concerns that the health care financing system can no longer do enough to cover Singaporeans for their old age. In 1980, the life expectancy of a Singaporean at age 65 years was 12.6 years for male and 15.4 years for female. By 2010, the projected life expectancy at age 65 years had increased to 18.1 years and 21.5 years for males and females respectively. The additional years lived often mean that they are faced with an extended period of required living expenses and most likely without a steady income stream. In addition, the system of social protection for older persons is weak due to the non-welfare philosophy of the Singapore government.

In 2010, the average Medisave account balance was $16,900; and 90% of Singaporeans were covered by MediShield and Integrated Shield Plan (see Fig. 2). However, this is far from the Medisave Minimum Sum (MMS)[2] stipulated by the government to ensure that Singaporeans have enough savings set aside to meet their future health care needs. In the year 2011, about six in 10 active members[3] have met the minimum sum at age 55. This means that a substantial proportion of the population is far from having sufficient savings for their health care needs.

While MediShield has been viewed as an important supplement to Medisave, the national insurance scheme is seeing cracks in its system. MediShield is an opt-out scheme; this means that the young and healthy have the choice of opting out and this will result in adverse selection. The annual premiums for MediShield can be paid from one's Medisave account, or by one's child. In 2007, the percentage of Singaporeans covered under MediShield or Integrated Shield Plans (ISPs) stood at 78% (see Fig. 2). The figure improved to 90% in 2010 following policy changes in December 2007 that sought to include the younger population into the insurance pool. The changes extended MediShield coverage to children of

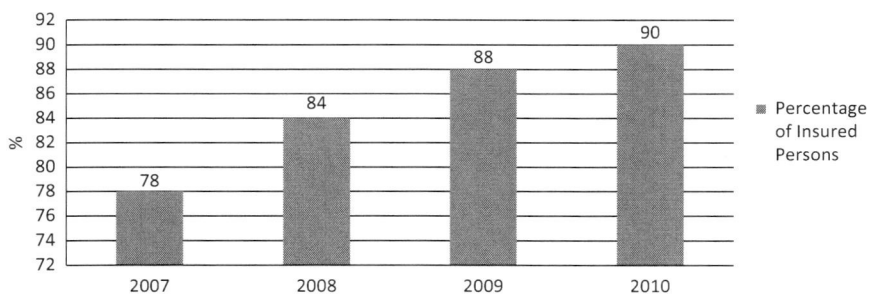

Figure 2. Percentage of Insured Persons (2007–2010).
Source: CPF trends, December 2011.

---

[2] As of 1 July 2012, the MMS was set at $38,500. This set figure is adjusted yearly.
[3] This is defined by CPF as persons who have at least one CPF contribution paid for them in any of the four months preceding their birth month.

Singapore citizens and Permanent Residents, thus effectively raising the percentage of insured persons.[4] Between 2007 and 2008, there was a six percentage point increase in coverage rates due to policy changes in the MediShield. This is decidedly an easy gain in raising the coverage rates, and essential in negating the problem of adverse selection by including the younger population. However, as MediShield remains an opt-out scheme, the concern remains that in the long run, there will be the attrition of the younger and healthier population, thus resulting in an "adverse pool" that may send MediShield into deficit.

The CPF Board has sought to mitigate this problem by age-adjusting the premiums of MediShield. This means that premiums for older persons are higher as they are expected to make more claims from the insurance pool. In the highest age-range, premiums for those aged 84–85 years are set at $1123. In contrast, those who are below 30 years pay $33 annually. While this is arguably justifiable as older persons are expected to dip more into the pool, the fact remains that the current generation of older persons[5] may not be able to afford such high premiums and may be forced to let their MediShield cover lapsed. This perpetuates the health inequality of older persons as it effectively inhibits their access to health.

This is also not expected to improve with the baby-boomer generation. In 2011, the average balance in the Medisave accounts of active CPF members at age 55 years was $29,928. At present value, the sum of MediShield premium from the age of 56–85 years would be $13,961. This means that older Singaporeans have a net of $15,967[6] after MediShield premiums for their health care expenditure if they stopped contributing to their CPF at age 55 years. The revamp of the MediShield in 2012 is laudable in that it recognizes the changing needs of an aging population. In view of the rising longevity of Singaporeans, the age ceiling for MediShield

---

[4] Previously, auto-coverage only kicked in upon first CPF contribution or registration of marriage. This essentially excluded most who are below 21 years of age.

[5] The current cohort of elderly have little savings in their CPF, as the amount they were required to set aside was low. Most of the current cohort of elderly were also in low-paying jobs due to their low educational level, and have little private savings set aside.

[6] The calculations are made at present values without factoring in CPF interest rates. Even if interest rates were factored in, the increase would be marginal at best.

coverage has been raised from 85 years to 90 years from January 2013. In addition, the lifetime claim limit for hospital expenses and certain outpatient treatment will be raised from $200,000 to $300,000.

Nonetheless, improved coverage inevitably means a higher premium deductible, and it is predicted that this is likely to hurt the poor and the elderly most. Premiums are expected to rise between $17 and $251, depending on a person's age group. The deductible is also expected to increase by $500 before patients can make claims from MediShield. This is expected to affect half of the Class C patients who now make MediShield claims but will no longer be able to do so once the changes kick in next year. In an attempt to sweeten the bitter pill, the government is offering all insured Singaporeans a one-off Medisave top-up of $50 to $400. In addition, about 85% of Singaporeans aged 66 years and above will get annual Medisave top-ups with amounts ranging between $250 and $450 through the GST Voucher Scheme. However, this does not negate the fact that the current revamp seems to perpetuate the situation of health inequalities for the poor and the elderly. The concern is that the poor and the elderly who tend to be income elastic may scale back on health care consumption such as delaying or even refusing treatment due to the price increase (or higher deductible). The income effect may therefore reduce the quantity of health care demanded by the poor and older persons; thus effectively containing national health care expenditure but perhaps at the consequence of health outcomes.

Data indicates that households with the lowest 20% income level spend about 6% of their monthly household expenditure on health care (see Table 3). In contrast, households in the highest quintile only spend about 4.8% of their monthly household expenditure on health care. The 1.2 percentage point difference may seem marginal, but it is indicative that low-income households have to spend a greater proportion of their income in order to receive health care. In translating it to the dollar value of health care consumed, it also shows that low-income households are unable to consume as much health care as high-income households.

Noteworthy is the sharp increase in Medifund disbursements over a period of five years from 2006 to 2010 (see Table 4). The total dollar value of approved applications to Medifund nearly doubled between 2006 and 2010. The increase can be partly explained by the growing number of

Table 3. Proportion of Monthly Household Expenditure Spent on Health care (%) by Income Quintiles.

	1997/1998	2002/2003	2007/2008
All Households	3.5	4.7	5.3
Lowest 20%	5	5.7	6
2nd quintile	3	4.8	5.5
3rd quintile	3.4	4.8	5.5
4th quintile	3.2	4.8	5.3
Highest quintile	3.3	4.1	4.8

Source: MOH.

Table 4. Medifund and Medifund Silver Grants to Medifund-approved Institutions.

	Restructured hospital/ Institutions ($ million)	Intermediate & Long-term care ($ million)	Total ($ million)	% Change in total
2006	37.7	3	40.7	—
2007	46.3	4	50.3	23.7
2008	66.3	7.4	73.7	46.5
2009	63.8	11.2	75	1.8
2010	68.6	12	80.6	7.5

Source: Medical Endowment Fund annual reports, various editions.

elderly Singaporeans who need financial aid for their basic health care. Secondly, Medifund Silver was extended in April 2008 to support all Medifund-approved institutions in the ILTC sector, thus explaining the 46.5% increase between 2007 and 2008. However, the figures indicate that more and more aged Singaporeans are unable to afford basic health care and are required to make applications to Medifund.

5. FINANCING ILTC IN THE FUTURE

The aging population will see increasing prevalence of chronic conditions such as dementia and osteoporosis rather than acute illnesses. This means that the delivery of health care will shift from episodic delivery (to intervene in an illness at a point in time) to the long-term management of chronic conditions as well as co-morbidities. This means that ILTC services such as day care, nursing homes and rehabilitative services will be in greater demand. Health systems therefore have to be able to provide a continuum of integrated health care services that allows for the decanting of care from the acute sector.

But unlike the acute sector, the ILTC sector has long been overlooked and the responsibility devolved toward private and non-profit operators. With an aging population, there is a growing recognition of the need to develop this sector for eldercare and restructure the payment method for the use of such services. At present, neither Medisave nor MediShield covers long-term care. ElderShield offers basic financial protection to those who need long-term care. Under this scheme, members receive a monthly payout of $400 for a maximum period of 72 months. However, this is inadequate as the need for long-term care more often spans more than a period of six years. For those who prefer to obtain higher coverage, ElderShield supplements offer higher monthly payouts and/or longer payout period are available. However, these do not come cheap, and are certainly not catered toward the elderly from low-income households. Although additional premiums are payable by Medisave, this is subjected to limits of $600 yearly and constrained by the amount that an individual has in his/her Medisave account. Moreover, for patients to file a claim to ElderShield, they have to fulfil the stringent criterion of being unable to do at least three of these six ADLs[7] — washing, dressing, feeding, toileting, mobility and transferring. This means that patients have to reach a very critical stage of dire health before they can tap into ElderShield funding. For needy and disabled elderly Singaporeans who are unable to join ElderShield because of their age or pre-existing disabilities, the IDAPE exists to help provide some form of subsidy. However, the disbursements are highly inadequate and only up to a maximum of 72 months. Under the IDAPE, applicants whose household per capita

---

[7] For individuals who choose to purchase ElderShield Supplements, some plans only require an individual to be unable to carry out two ADLs out of the six before they are eligible for a claim.

income is $1501–$2200 receive $150 monthly; applicants whose household per capita income is $1500 and below receive $250 monthly.

Low-income elderly are entitled to appeal to Medifund for subsidies, and the percentage of the bill subsidized is calibrated according to an individual's household per capita income level (see Table 5). The co-payment element of the bill means that a portion of the individual's intermediate and long-term care expenditure is still out-of-pocket. The final out-of-pocket amount payable ranges as VWOs offer varying charges according to their organizations' funding ability. However, as VWOs price at the level of normal costing or the lowest possible price according to their funding ability (commonly referred to as blind subsidy, this means that all enrolled patients into the nursing home receive a discounted price regardless of their income level), the fees are arguably manageable and VWOs are often willing to help and/or strike a negotiation with truly low-income patients who are in need of help. However, a tricky situation exists for patients under the portable subsidy scheme. Since April 2003, the MOH introduced the portable subsidy scheme in the wake of the chronic shortage of

Table 5. Subsidy Rates for ILTC Facilities (Excluding Community Hospitals).

Per capita monthly household income	Subsidy level for residential services* (excluding community hospitals)		Subsidy level for home and community-based services† (non-residential services)	
	Singapore citizens (%)	Permanent residents (%)	Singapore citizens (%)	Permanent residents (%)
$0 to $600	75	50	80	55
$601 to $900	60	40	75	50
$901 to $1300	50	30	60	40
$1301 to $1500	40	20	50	30
$1501 to $2200	20	10	30	15
$2201 and above	0	0	0	0

Source: AIC.
* These include nursing homes, hospitals for the chronically sick, inpatient hospices, and rehabilitation homes and sheltered homes for those who were mentally ill.
† These includes day rehabilitation centres, dementia day care centres, day rehabilitation for those who were mentally ill, hospice home medical, hospice home nursing, home medical and home nursing.

bed space in VWOs-operated nursing homes. This means that accredited private nursing homes can set aside a certain proportion of their beds for patients who are eligible for MOH subsidies and referred to by the AIC. For means-tested patients under the portable subsidy scheme, the out-of-pocket expenditure however becomes substantial as private nursing homes charge at a market rate. This easily amounts up to a few hundred dollars depending on the functional status of the patient and the type of hospital ward (defined by the number of beds in a room) that the patient selects. Although the portable subsidy scheme was well-intended at reducing the waiting time for a space in nursing homes, it could have led to an unintended effect.

6. DISCUSSION

The Singapore health care system is perhaps an enigma to many nations out there that struggle to contain their health care expenditure while offering an advanced health care system. The national health care expenditure has long stood at 3%–4% of Singapore's GDP. Yet, the little island state has managed to put together a system that is worthy of international accolades for its performance. In a 2000 World Health Organization (WHO) study of world's health systems, Singapore was ranked sixth out of 191 countries on health systems performance. More recently, the International Institute of Management Development (IMD) World Competitiveness Yearbook ranked Singapore's health infrastructure third out of 55 countries. Vis-à-vis the average spending level of the Organization for Economic Co-operation and Development (OECD) nations — that stands at about 9.5% of their GDP, Singapore's health care spending is significantly low. This may be attributed to the fact that many OECD nations are welfare states, and the state provides health care services directly to their citizens. However, the success of public health policies as well as social and economic development in many nations across the world have given rise to the global phenomenon of population aging. This is set to put many health care systems across the world under stress as they strive to cope with the growing demand for health care that comes from an aging population.

Likewise, Singapore is set to meet with the challenge of an aging population. In 2011, 9.3% of its population was aged 65 years and above.

By 2030, it is estimated that they will form 18.7% of the population. This growth in the elderly population was expected to escalate when the first batch of baby-boomers turned 65 years in 2012, and this would mark the beginning of a rapid phase of Singapore's demographic transition into a society with a significant elderly population. The Singapore health care system is set to face a critical test as the aging population will consume more health care. This is expected to require more health care facilities, services and personnel to meet the demands of an aging population, and total health care expenditure is inevitably set to rise.

The Singapore government's resistance to a welfare state is renowned. Its founding Prime Minister Lee Kuan Yew's view on the matter has greatly shaped the policy formulation milieu in Singapore — "Welfare undermined self-reliance. People did not have to work for their families' well-being. The hand-out became a way of life." Health care in Singapore is therefore not free, rather the nation's health care financing system functions on the twin philosophies of individual responsibility and affordable health care for all.

However, the health care sector does not and should not function on pure market forces alone. Adam Smith's theory of the invisible hand posits that the actions of self-interested buyers and sellers will result in the most efficient allocation of resources. Market prices perform two important functions — first, it can act as a rationing function, second, it has an allocative function. The rationing function of price distributes resources to consumers who value them most highly; the allocative function of price directs resources away from overcrowded markets to markets that are underserved. However, the invisible hand does not guarantee equitable distribution of the goods and services produced. In the case of health care, society's notions of social justice often create an aversion and prohibit the allocation of health care resources based on price alone.

As Amartya Sen rightly puts, "Health is among the most important conditions of human life and a critically significant constituent of human capabilities which we have reason to value". Yet, the persistence of health inequalities across the world today remains an endemic problem. Notions of social justice call for these health inequalities to be equalized. However questions of "what", "how" and "to what extent" health inequalities can be equalized are proving difficult to answer. The preamble to the WHO's

Constitution provides a useful clue on what may be done toward achieving health equity, in which it recognizes that "the enjoyment of the *highest attainable* standard of health is one of the fundamental rights of every human being". The term "*highest attainable*" rightly encapsulates the ideal of the highest standard of health within the means of rational use of health care resources.

Health equity is however not confined to the distribution of health care resources, but entails a broader discussion on the socioeconomic determinants of health. To speak about health equity purely in terms of equal health status outcomes is also unrealistic and impossible. Health status outcomes are a complex confluence of factors such as gender, genes, lifestyle habits, environment and income. The aspiration toward equal health status for all will unfortunately be an elusive concept.

However, it is imperative that social arrangements such as subsidies and transfers still exist to ensure that there are opportunities to health. How should this be achieved? Perhaps we may take the position of John Rawl's theory of social justice. The Rawlsian principle states that "social and economic inequalities are to be arranged to the greatest benefit of the least advantaged". In a society like Singapore, which eschews the welfare state, this is in fact the approach undertaken by the government to ensure that no Singaporean gets left behind, in differentiating the concept of equity as opposed to equality.

The co-payment policy was instituted by the government to prevent moral hazard. This stemmed from founding Prime Minister Lee Kuan Yew's early experience with citizenry behavior contributing to the waste incurred when free health care was provided in the British National Health Service. The co-payment policy thus functions as a form of gate-keeping against overconsumption of health care. However, this has become a catch-22 situation in which the policy intending to curtail wastage has led to over-rationing of medical resources to patients who are truly in need of them. The co-payment policy has thus become an inhibition to the poor seeking medical treatment or rehabilitation. This has been deemed detrimental to the health status of the poor as they delay medical treatment and spiral into more critical conditions; or medical rehabilitation that is pivotal to a full recovery is not sought and patients relapse.

7. CONCLUSION

The fundamental economic problem thus crops up in health resource allocation — how to meet unlimited wants with limited means? Unlike many governments in the world that are struggling to contain their health care expenditure, the Singapore government is in an enviable position of being able to increase its health care budget. In the 2012 Budget, the Singapore government pledged to double health care expenditure from $4 billion to $8 billion over the next five years. The increased budget will be aimed at ramping up health care capacity, increasing health care affordability and paying health care professionals more competitively. Credit has to be given to the Singapore government for finally recognizing the need of addressing health care affordability, particularly for the "sandwich" class.

The government however, has reiterated the importance of maintaining a balance in public finances, while cautioning against continual expansion of social entitlements. The need to adhere to a system of sustainable finances where the nation spends what it can afford remains a cornerstone of Singapore's policymaking. However, it should also be noted that there is a limit to what government transfers can do for the lower-income. The Gini coefficient in 2011 was 0.473 for Singapore, which stands as one of the highest in the World. Even with government transfers and taxes factored in, the Gini coefficient is marginally mitigated to 0.452. Inequities in the health sector cannot be adequately tackled without concomitant changes in the overall income distribution of national wealth. This has to be balanced by strengthening government roles in the financing and provision of public goods, judicious interventions to address market failures in health care, and especially more for the growing aging population.

8. COMMENTS ON PRESENTATION BY SPEAKER

Discussant: Ms Lim Sia Hoe, General Manager

NTUC Eldercare Co-operative Limited

The biggest misconception I have come across is the belief that our eldercare services sector is in good shape because of our comprehensive health care systems in Medisave, MediShield, and Medifund (collectively the "3Ms"). Alas! the reality is that "3M" funds cannot be widely used to finance eldercare services given the needless distinction drawn between eldercare and health care. Those needing or wanting eldercare services in the form of day care services, homecare services, assisted living facilities, or wellness programs, therefore have few avenues to turn to for financial assistance. Many end up digging deep into their own pockets or are forced to regard such services as unaffordable luxuries, which is a real pity.

While there is no denying the key role the "3Ms" play in helping one cope with the medical costs of aging, eldercare support remains equally important in the promotion of active aging and holistic wellbeing. The sad truth is that even though Singapore is rapidly aging,[8] there is currently little being set aside to develop equally comprehensive eldercare support systems. Save for ElderShield insurance, there is no other "Es" that an individual can leverage on. The marginal 0.5% increase in CPF contribution to the Medisave accounts (from Budget 2012) is hardly sufficient to guard against the rising health care costs while the Eldercare Fund and the CST are targeted at institutions rather than individuals directly. Much is left to these institutions to allocate the resources as they so desire, which is hardly ideal.

Financial support against old age should not be simply confined to the polyclinics or hospitals wards, or only be made available to the severely disabled.[9] Aging begins far earlier and active aging particularly encompasses so much more. An estimated 42,000 seniors in Singapore today require assistance with at least one ADL.[10] About 9800 (or 23%) of them receive institutional care, and the remaining 32,200 are cared for in the community. With an increasing life expectancy and a decreasing Total Fertility Rate (TFR), the burden of eldercare costs on families and society will steadily increase. We will also see more elderly living alone and more elderly households grappling with the demands of age (see Table 6). The problem is thus right at the doorstep, and inching closer to home every day.

Hence, as the eldercare sector develops a continuum of services to cater to the differing needs at every stage of aging, there is a genuine need to supplement them with adequate funding support. Much like the "3M" model, the umbrella framework should be designed to cover eldercare over

---

[8] One in 11 Singaporeans, or 335,300 Singaporeans, were aged 65 and above in 2010. By 2020, the proportion will increase to one in seven Singaporeans, or 587,300 Singaporeans.
[9] A person must have a minimum of three ADLs to qualify for ElderShield.
[10] The six ADLs are bathing, toileting, dressing, eating, transferring, and mobility.

Table 6. 2010 and Projected Care Needs of Seniors*.

	2010 (335,300)	2020 (587,300)
Seniors who require assistance in at least one ADL in the community	32,200 (9.7%)	56,968
Seniors cared for by family, friends, flatmates (who require assistance in ADLs)	15,500 (4.6%)	27,015
Seniors cared for by FDWs[†] (who require assistance in ADLs)	9000 (2.6%)	15,269
Seniors with no caregivers (who require assistance in ADLs)	7700 (2.3%)	13,508
Seniors with dementia	20,000	40,000 (assuming 2X increase from 2010, due to more older old)
Seniors who utilize day centres	3800 (1.12%)	6577
Seniors who utilize home help services	2300 (0.7%)	4111

*Using simple linear extrapolation.
[†] Foreign domestic workers.

the long term, and cater not just for the low-income households but also for those households who fall through the cracks.

This necessitates a fundamental rethink of our eldercare policies. A good first step would be to expand the "3Ms" to cover eldercare services in recognition that health care and eldercare are but two sides of the same coin. At the same time, we should consider developing our own all-inclusive individual-centric "3Es" framework to empower more people with access to such services so that they can enjoy their golden years to the best of their ability and with peace of mind.

8.1. Explanatory Notes

8.1.1. *Eldercare fund*

Eldercare Fund is an endowment fund set up in 2000 with an initial capital of $200 million. Further capital injections will be made when budget surpluses are available. The interest income from the Fund will be used to finance operating subsidies to nursing homes run by VWOs.

The government increased the capital sum of the Eldercare Fund from $1 billion to $2.5 billion in 2010. The Eldercare Fund will also be extended to provide subsidies for the entire range of elderly and continuing care.

As announced by Prime Minister Lee Hsien Loong in his 2010 National Day Rally speech, the government has decided that the Eldercare Fund should also cover community hospitals, hospices, day rehabilitation, home medical, and home nursing care, in addition to nursing homes. The capital sum should then be sufficient for operating subsidies to the entire range of elderly, and continuing care facilities and services will be fully financed from the interest income of the Fund.

8.1.2. *CST*

The CST is a dollar-for-dollar donation-matching grant provided by the government to enhance the services of VWOs in the ILTC sector.

One key objective of the CST is to encourage public donations from philanthropists, other organizations, and also the man in the street. VWOs need donations from the public for their day-to-day operations. With additional CST funds matched by the government, VWOs will be able to enhance their capabilities and also expand their capacities to improve quality of care for their clients.

Jointly managed by the MOH and the Ministry of Community Development, Youth and Sports (MCYS), the CST is administered by the AIC for the health sector, while National Council of Social Service (NCSS) administers for the social service sector.

REFERENCES

Access Economics (2006). Dementia in the Asia Pacific region: The Epidemic is Here. Report, Alzheimer's Disease International. http://www.alz.co.uk/research/files/apreport.

Lim, MK (2004). Shifting the burden of health care finance: A case study of public–private partnership in Singapore. *Health Policy*, 69, 83–92.

Ling, SL (1998). Health care of the elderly in Singapore. *Singapore Medical Journal*, 39(10), 435–436. http://www.sma.org.sg/smj/3910/articles.

Ng, TP, M Niti, PC Chiam and EH Kua (2006). Prevalence and correlates of functional disability in multiethnic elderly Singaporeans. *Journal of American Geriatrics Society*, 54(1), 21–29.

Phua, KH (2002). The savings approach to financing long-term care in Singapore. *Journal of Aging and Social Policy*, 13, 169–183.

Singapore Committee on Ageing Issues (2013). Demographic realities. *Report on the Ageing Population*. Singapore: Ministry of Social and Family Development. http://app.msf.gov.sg/portals/summary/research.

Singapore Department of Statistics (2012). *Population Trends 2012*. http://www.singstat.gov.sg/publications.

Singapore Inter-Ministerial Committee on Ageing (1999). *Inter-Ministerial Committee Report on the Ageing Population 1999*. Singapore: Ministry of Social and Family Development. http://app.msf.gov.sg/Publications/IMC-Report-on-the-Ageing-Population.

Singapore Ministerial Committee on Ageing (2012). Committee of supply 2012 speech by Minister Gan Kim Yong. http://www.moh.gov.sg/content/moh_web/home/pressRoom/speeches_d/2012/COS_speech_by_Mini_ster_Gan_on_MCA_initiatives.html.

Singapore Ministry of Community, Youth and Sports (2012). Committee of supply 2012 speech by Minister of State. http://app.msf.gov.sg/Press-Room/COS-2012-Debates-MOS-Halimah-Yacob-Speech.

Singapore Ministry of Health (2012a). Committee of supply 2012 speech by Minister of State for Health on ILTC manpower initiatives. http://www.moh.gov.sg/content/moh_web/home/pressRoom/speeches_d/2012/COS_speech_by_Mini_ster_Of_State_for_Health_ILTC_Manpower_Initiatives.html.

Singapore Ministry of Health (2012b). More affordable intermediate and long-term care services to help Singaporeans age-in-place. http://www.moh.gov.sg/content/moh_web/home/pressRoom/pressRoomItemRelease/2012/more_aff_ordable_intermediateandlongtermcareservicestohelpsingap.html.

Singapore Ministry of Health (2012c). Subsidies for government-funded intermediate long-term care services. http://www.moh.gov.sg/content/moh_web/home/costs_and_financing/schemes_subsides/subsides_f_or_government_funded_ILTC_services.html.

Singapore Ministry of Health (2013). Committee of supply 2013 speech by Minister for Health on better health for all. http://www.moh.gov.sg/content/moh_web/home/pressRoom/speeches_d/2013/MOH2013COSMinSpeechBetterHealthforAllPart2of2.html.

Singapore Ministry of Health (n.d.) ElderShield webpage. http://www.moh.gov.sg/content/moh_web/home/costs_and_financing/schemes_subsidies/ElderShield.html.

CHAPTER 7

HOUSING AFFORDABILITY
Is Housing Still Affordable?: New Disaggregated Indicators

SPEAKER: ASSOCIATE PROFESSOR LUM SAU KIM
*Department of Real Estate and Institute of Real Estate Studies,
National University of Singapore*

MS ZHOU XUEFENG
Institute of Real Estate Studies, National University of Singapore

1. INTRODUCTION

Over the past few years, housing affordability has been a key policy concern in Singapore due to the pronounced price inflation of housing assets pre- and post-financial crisis. Figure 1 shows that from July 2005 to November 2007, nominal house prices appreciated 73% as measured by the National University of Singapore (NUS) Singapore Residential Price Index (SRPI). The private housing market subsequently declined 22% and hit a post-crisis low in March 2009 before rebounding about 51% by July 2012. These movements are also broadly reflected by the Urban Redevelopment Authority (URA) Private Residential Price Index which appreciated 84% from its last trough in the first quarter of 2004 to the second quarter of 2012. In the secondary public housing market, capital appreciation as measured by the Housing and Development Board (HDB) Resale Price Index was equally dramatic: prices rose 92% between mid-2005 and mid-2012 with only a 1% fall in the first quarter of 2009.

Figure 1. Housing Price Movements in Singapore (Q4: 2001 = 100).

To allay concerns about housing affordability, policymakers have relied on two sets of statistics. The first compared the growth rates of the median household income and the HDB Resale Price Index between 1999 and 2009 while a subsequent study computed the prevailing debt service ratio of the monthly loan instalment to the gross monthly income of households that had bought new suburban HDB flats.[1] By focusing on the median or on households who have already purchased new flats, both studies do not provide a holistic view of housing affordability across the entire distribution of households for different housing options. This chapter directly addresses this gap by analysing the ability of households across the income spectrum to afford a range of public and suburban private housing. Specifically, we compute the house price to household income multiple by decile cohorts over time to track the impact of price movements on housing affordability. This approach not only generates a more robust measure of housing affordability but also draws attention to potential gaps in affordability across different household income groups.

---

[1] These were reported in *The Straits Times* on 7 April 2010 and 27 April 2012, respectively.

The next section provides a brief review of the literature relating to the measurement of housing affordability. Our methodology and the data used, including public and private housing price data from 2000 to 2011, are described in the sections on methodology and data, respectively. The section on housing affordability presents our indicators and compares the disaggregated and aggregated approaches, followed by the conclusion.

2. LITERATURE REVIEW

Housing affordability measures are important and useful indicators to assess whether government policies are effective in delivering what was intended to be achieved (Kazakevitch and Borrowman, 2009). To accurately reflect the markets being evaluated, various indicators of housing affordability have been offered by academics, researchers, lending agencies, and policymakers that help identify the magnitude and nature of housing affordability problems and their geographic distribution. Many studies have employed variants of the conventional housing affordability model commonly referred to as the housing expenditure-to-income approach that measures the ratio of what households pay for their housing to what they earn (Kamath, 1988; Hancock, 1993).This method often specifies the level of the median free-market price of a dwelling unit relative to the median annual household income, although averages are sometimes used as well. Another measure popular with lending institutions is the debt service ratio which assesses the affordability levels of borrowers in terms of loan servicing capability. A rule of thumb in underwriting is that no more than 25% to 30% of a household's monthly income should be spent as monthly housing cost.

In recent years, new measures of housing affordability have been proposed that are more informative than the conventional measures of central tendency (Burke, 2003; Robinson *et al.*, 2006; Ndubueze, 2007; Abeyshinghe and Gu, 2011; Kazakevitch and Borrowman, 2009). By capturing a wider dimension of problems than traditional indicators, they offer fresh insights into understanding the breadth and depth of housing affordability issues. In particular, Gan and Hill (2009) introduced a form of disaggregated measure that emphasizes the entire distribution of household incomes and house prices and not just the medians. Since differential skewness in the house price and income distributions can cause median price-to-income ratios to significantly understate the extent of the housing affordability problem for lower income households, taking account of other quantiles generates a more robust measure of housing affordability by ensuring that the resulting affordability index is representative of the whole distribution of quantile ratios.

We adopt the measures introduced by Gan and Hill (2009) as our interest is to determine if any income groups are relatively underserved. Unlike other studies that focus on the accessibility of private housing to HDB upgraders (Yuen *et al.*, 2006) or upward mobility from the public to private housing sector (Ong, 2000), we examine the affordability of both public and private housing options. Our work is similar in flavor to that of Abeyshinghe and Gu (2011), which determined housing affordability across age cohorts. However, we compute the price to income multiple across income cohorts rather than the ratio of predicted lifetime income to house price for different age groups.

3. METHODOLOGY

This study will adopt the Gan and Hill (2009) model of looking beyond the median. We extend the conventional measure of computing the ratio of house price to annual household income using the median to every decile of the household income and house price distributions.

Let $g(x)$ and $f(y)$ denote the probability density functions of annual household income and house price, respectively. x_q and y_q refer to the income and house price at the qth quantile of their distributions (where $q \in [0, 1]$), respectively. For example, $x_{0.5}$ and $y_{0.5}$ are the median values of x and y. Hence, letting x_q and y_q denote the qth quantile values of $g(x)$ and $f(y)$ respectively, we obtain

$$\int_{x_0}^{x_q} g(x)dx = \int_{y_0}^{y_q} f(y)dy = q$$

It is possible to calculate $AaQ(q)$ or housing affordability at quantile q as follows:

$$AaQ(q) = y_q / x_q$$

An increase in AaQ (q) implies reduced affordability for that particular quantile. For example, the median price-to-income ratio AaQ (0.5) is used by Demographia International (2008) to measure housing affordability across regions and cities. Various real estate institutes and government agencies in the US and Australia have employed the median price-to-income ratio of AaQ (0.5) to provide affordability indexes. They include the National Association of Realtors (NAR), the US Department of Housing and Urban Development (HUD), Commonwealth Bank of Australia (CBA) and Housing Industry Association (HIA). Similar housing affordability indexes have also been employed by Phang (2009), Mah (2009), Chan (2009) and DTZ (2010) in Singapore.

We compute and plot affordability ratios denoted by AaD (d) for each decile from 2000 to 2011. For example, AaD (1) refers to housing affordability at the 1st or lowest decile. The ratios are computed annually for the sample period 2000 to 2011 for new and resale four-room HDB flats as well as suburban private residential properties captured in the SRPI database. Executive condominiums and other flat types are excluded as we have incomplete data samples while prime residential properties are omitted as the affordability of this segment is not a key policy concern.

4. DATA

This section presents the distributions of household income and prices of new and resale HDB flats and private suburban residential properties by decile.

4.1. Household Income

Household income data is obtained from the Department of Statistics. Table 1 presents the annual household income from work for each decile of the household income distribution and includes employer Central Provident Fund (CPF) contributions. The annual median household income is shown separately in Table 2.

Figure 2 plots the data. While household income for the top decile experienced the greatest growth over our sample period, the household

Table 1. Average Annual Household Income by Decile.

Deciles	2000	2001	2002	2003	2004	2005	2006	2007	2008	2009	2010	2011
1st–10th	$16,584	$15,972	$15,192	$14,676	$14,784	$15,084	$15,096	$15,852	$16,788	$16,332	$17,964	$18,972
11th–20th	$26,892	$27,300	$26,160	$25,968	$26,388	$27,084	$27,660	$29,016	$32,400	$32,352	$35,280	$37,620
21st–30th	$35,832	$36,516	$35,328	$35,808	$35,856	$37,392	$38,184	$40,548	$45,972	$45,444	$49,896	$53,052
31st–40th	$44,196	$46,404	$44,664	$44,952	$45,432	$48,240	$48,456	$52,020	$58,872	$59,736	$65,016	$69,528
41st–50th	$54,060	$56,160	$54,864	$55,644	$55,776	$58,308	$59,652	$64,296	$72,660	$71,760	$79,236	$84,384
51st–60th	$63,648	$68,124	$66,264	$67,656	$66,048	$70,380	$72,324	$78,732	$89,904	$87,828	$94,080	$101,232
61st–70th	$76,248	$81,012	$79,968	$80,700	$79,596	$85,632	$86,160	$95,136	$107,484	$105,576	$111,720	$121,212
71st–80th	$91,296	$99,864	$97,584	$98,748	$96,144	$103,692	$105,708	$113,748	$129,840	$128,328	$133,260	$147,672
81st–90th	$113,532	$129,060	$123,528	$123,252	$124,200	$128,412	$132,576	$148,632	$168,156	$161,076	$167,316	$186,108
91st–100th	$191,352	$209,604	$203,976	$205,752	$209,916	$216,912	$229,200	$253,752	$287,616	$274,908	$293,304	$334,404

Table 2. Annual Median Household Income.

	2000	2001	2002	2003	2004	2005	2006	2007	2008	2009	2010	2011
Median	$52,776	$56,592	$55,080	$55,344	$54,624	$57,972	$59,424	$64,344	$73,200	$72,072	$76,104	$84,444

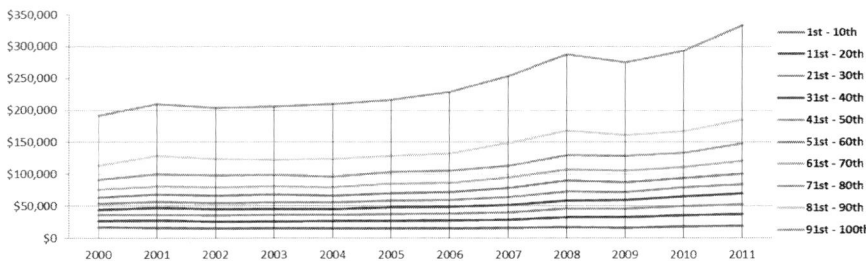

Figure 2. Average Annual Household Income by Decile Over Time.

Table 3. Key Statistics for Average Annual Household Income by Decile.

Deciles	Spread[a] (2000 to 2011)	Percentage Change[b] (2000 to 2011)	Average (Over the 12-Year Period)	Maximum (Year)	Minimum (Year)
1st–10th	$2388	14%	$16,108	$18,972 (2011)	$14,676 (2003)
11th–20th	$10,728	40%	$29,510	$37,620 (2011)	$25,968 (2003)
21st–30th	$17,220	48%	$40,819	$53,052 (2011)	$35,328 (2002)
31st–40th	$25,332	57%	$52,293	$69,528 (2011)	$44,196 (2000)
41st–50th	$30,324	56%	$63,900	$84,384 (2011)	$54,060 (2000)
51st–60th	$37,584	59%	$77,185	$101,232 (2011)	$63,648 (2000)
61st–70th	$44,964	59%	$92,537	$121,212 (2011)	$76,248 (2000)
71st–80th	$56,376	62%	$112,157	$147,672 (2011)	$91,296 (2000)
81st–90th	$72,576	64%	$142,154	$186,108 (2011)	$113,532 (2000)
91st–100th	$143,052	75%	$242,558	$334,404 (2011)	$191,352 (2000)

[a] Spread = Average annual household income in 2011 — Average annual household income in 2000.
[b] Percentage change = Spread / Average annual household income in 2000.

income of the bottom decile remained fairly constant. This suggests that the income gap between the lowest and the highest deciles has been widening over the past 11 years. In percentage terms, Table 3 shows that incomes grew 14% for the first decile while the highest decile saw a 75% increase in household income. From 2000 to 2011, the average annual household income for the 1st decile is $16,108 as compared to $242,558 for the 10th decile.

4.2. Prices of New HDB Flats

We derive the prices of new HDB flats from the price range stated in the various HDB Annual Reports and present the data as well as other key statistics in Tables 4 and 5. As only the maximum and minimum prices are reported, we have assumed a uniform distribution of house price within each decile. Note that our prices have taken into account the Additional CPF Housing Grant (AHG) provided by the government to eligible buyers of new flats. The AHG typically ranges from $5000 to $40,000, depending on the average monthly income level of a household, and is used to offset the purchase price of a flat and reduce the housing loan that a flat buyer needs to take. Based on the HDB Annual Report's "Key Statistics FY 2010/2011", we have assumed that buyers of four-room flats were typically given an AHG of $10,000.

Figure 3 plots the data and shows that the prices of new HDB flats have generally appreciated over the sample period with a marked spike in 2009 for most deciles. The spread and the percentage change in prices for new HDB four-room flats from 2000 to 2011 are shown in Table 5. Compared to household income, the percentage change of new HDB flat prices for all deciles are significantly larger. While household incomes appreciated between 14 and 79%, new HDB flat prices increased by 71% to 167%.

4.3. Prices of Resale HDB Flats

The prices of resale HDB flats are derived from resale transactions and computed in a similar manner to those of new HDB flats. Resale price data is only available from 2001 onwards.

The price dynamics is evident from Fig. 4. Across all deciles, resale flat prices stayed flat from 2001 to 2006 but grew strongly in 2007 and 2008. The growth was relatively slower in 2009 due to the global financial crisis but prices surged again in 2010 and 2011. Comparing the prices of resale and new flats in Tables 5 and 6, resale flats cost about 54% to 90.6% higher than new HDB flats with the difference being more significant for the more expensive flats.

Table 4. Prices of New HDB Four-Room Flats by Decile.

Deciles	2000	2001	2002	2003	2004	2005	2006	2007	2008	2009	2010	2011
1st–10th	$111,910	$87,930	$87,030	$92,070	$92,050	$109,020	$122,070	$122,050	$125,070	$174,080	$193,020	$191,040
11th–20th	$114,720	$96,160	$95,360	$100,840	$102,600	$118,240	$131,840	$135,600	$138,840	$189,960	$206,240	$210,480
21st–30th	$117,530	$104,390	$103,690	$109,610	$113,150	$127,460	$141,610	$149,150	$152,610	$205,840	$219,460	$229,920
31st–40th	$120,340	$112,620	$112,020	$118,380	$123,700	$136,680	$151,380	$162,700	$166,380	$221,720	$232,680	$249,360
41st–50th	$123,150	$120,850	$120,350	$127,150	$134,250	$145,900	$161,150	$176,250	$180,150	$237,600	$245,900	$268,800
51st–60th	$125,960	$129,080	$128,680	$135,920	$144,800	$155,120	$170,920	$189,800	$193,920	$253,480	$259,120	$288,240
61st–70th	$128,770	$137,310	$137,010	$144,690	$155,350	$164,340	$180,690	$203,350	$207,690	$269,360	$272,340	$307,680
71st–80th	$131,580	$145,540	$145,340	$153,460	$165,900	$173,560	$190,460	$216,900	$221,460	$285,240	$285,560	$327,120
81st–90th	$134,390	$153,770	$153,670	$162,230	$176,450	$182,780	$200,230	$230,450	$235,230	$301,120	$298,780	$346,560
91st–100th	$137,200	$162,000	$162,000	$171,000	$187,000	$192,000	$210,000	$244,000	$249,000	$317,000	$312,000	$366,000

Table 5. Key Statistics for Average Annual Household Income by Decile.

Deciles	Spread[c] (2000 to 2011)	Percentage Change[d] (2000 to 2011)	Average (Over The 12-Year Period)	Maximum (Year)	Minimum (Year)
1st–10th	$79,130	71%	$125,612	$193,020 (2010)	$87,030 (2002)
11th–20th	$95,760	83%	$136,740	$210,480 (2011)	$95,360 (2002)
21st–30th	$112,390	96%	$147,868	$229,920 (2011)	$103,690 (2002)
31st–40th	$129,020	107%	$158,997	$249,360 (2011)	$112,020 (2002)
41st–50th	$145,650	118%	$170,125	$268,800 (2011)	$120,350 (2002)
51st–60th	$162,280	129%	$181,253	$288,240 (2011)	$125,960 (2000)
61st–70th	$178,910	139%	$192,382	$307,680 (2011)	$128,770 (2000)
71st–80th	$195,540	149%	$203,510	$327,120 (2011)	$131,580 (2000)
81st–90th	$212,170	158%	$214,638	$346,560 (2011)	$134,390 (2000)
91st–100th	$228,800	167%	$225,767	$366,000 (2011)	$137,200 (2000)

[c]Spread = Prices of new HDB flats in 2011 — Prices of new HDB flats in 2000.
[d]Percentage change = Spread / Prices of new HDB flats in 2000.

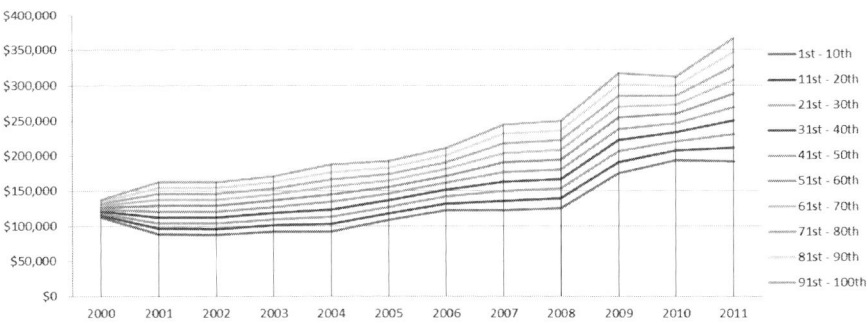

Figure 3. Prices of New HDB Four-Room Flats by Decile Over Time.

4.4. Prices of Private Residential Properties

In this study, our sample of private residential properties comprises non-landed and completed[2] private residential projects in the non-central region. The definition of non-central region used here is based on the definition

---

[2] In SRPI, all projects were completed before October 2011.

Table 6. Prices of Resale HDB Four-Room Flats by Decile.

Deciles	2001	2002	2003	2004	2005	2006	2007	2008	2009	2010	2011
1st (lowest)	$151,800	$148,211	$151,264	$173,314	$166,250	$165,000	$173,200	$191,765	$229,400	$270,200	$307,406
11th–20th	$171,611	$169,450	$171,880	$192,866	$186,428	$186,818	$203,632	$225,765	$260,338	$304,186	$344,288
21st–30th	$191,422	$190,688	$192,497	$212,418	$206,606	$208,635	$234,064	$259,766	$291,276	$338,171	$381,170
31st–40th	$211,233	$211,927	$213,113	$231,970	$226,784	$230,453	$264,496	$293,766	$322,214	$372,157	$418,051
41st–50th	$231,044	$233,165	$233,729	$251,522	$246,962	$252,270	$294,928	$327,767	$353,152	$406,143	$454,933
51st–60th	$250,856	$254,404	$254,346	$271,074	$267,139	$274,088	$325,361	$361,767	$384,091	$440,128	$491,815
61st–70th	$270,667	$275,642	$274,962	$290,626	$287,317	$295,905	$355,793	$395,768	$415,029	$474,114	$528,697
71st–80th	$290,478	$296,881	$295,578	$310,178	$307,495	$317,723	$386,225	$429,768	$445,967	$508,100	$565,578
81st–90th	$310,289	$318,119	$316,195	$329,730	$327,673	$339,540	$416,657	$463,769	$476,905	$542,085	$602,460
10th (highest)	$330,100	$339,358	$336,811	$349,282	$347,851	$361,358	$447,089	$497,769	$507,843	$576,071	$639,342

Table 7. Key Statistics for Prices of Resale HDB Four-Room Flats by Decile.

Deciles	Spread[e] (2001 to 2011)	Percentage change[f] (2001 to 2011)	Average (Over The 11-Year Period)	Maximum (Year)	Minimum (Year)
1st (lowest)	$155,606	103%	$193,437	$307,406 (2011)	$148,211 (2002)
11th–20th	$172,677	101%	$219,751	$344,288 (2011)	$169,450 (2002)
21st–30th	$189,747	99%	$246,065	$381,170 (2011)	$190,688 (2002)
31st–40th	$206,818	98%	$272,379	$418,051 (2011)	$211,233 (2001)
41st–50th	$223,889	97%	$298,692	$454,933 (2011)	$231,044 (2001)
51st–60th	$240,959	96%	$325,006	$491,815 (2011)	$250,856 (2001)
61st–70th	$258,030	95%	$351,320	$528,697 (2011)	$270,667 (2001)
71st–80th	$275,101	95%	$377,634	$565,578 (2011)	$290,478 (2001)
81st–90th	$292,171	94%	$403,947	$602,460 (2011)	$310,289 (2001)
10th (highest)	$309,242	94%	$430,261	$639,342 (2011)	$330,100 (2001)

[e]Spread = Prices of resale HDB flats in 2011 – Prices of resale HDB flats in 2001.
[f]Percentage change = Spread / Prices of resale HDB flats in 2001.

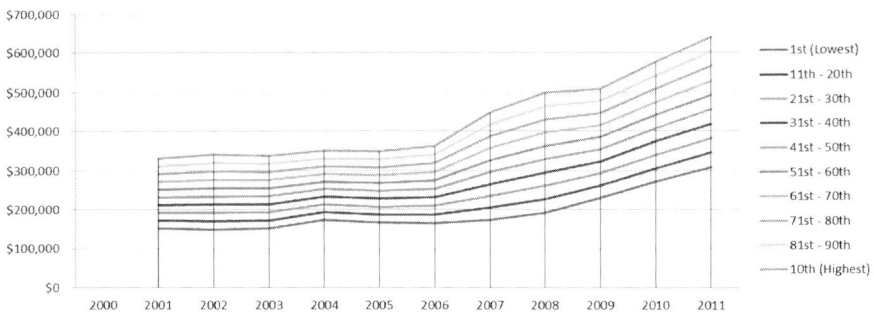

Figure 4. Prices of Resale HDB Four-Room Flats by Decile Over Time.

used for the SRPI, which excludes units in postal districts 1 to 4 and 9 to 11. The data source is URA Real Estate Information System (REALIS).

Unlike public housing prices, which bottomed between 2000 and 2002, private house prices had their troughs in 2004, except for the 1st decile that bottomed in 2005. Private residential prices were also more volatile compared to the prices of HDB flats. Table 8 shows the price volatilities from 2000 to 2011.

146 Inequality in Singapore

Table 8. Percentage Change of Private Residential by Decile.

Deciles	Percentage change (2000 to 2004) (%)	Percentage change (2004 to 2007) (%)	Percentage change (2007 to 2009) (%)	Percentage change (2009 to 2011) (%)
1st–10th	−18	24	13	9
11th–10th	−16	42	3	13
21st–30th	−16	55	−3	15
31st–40th	−15	65	−6	17
41st–50th	−14	73	−9	19
51st–60th	−14	80	−11	20
61st–70th	−13	85	−13	21
71st–80th	−13	90	−14	22
81st–90th	−13	94	−15	23
91st–100th	−12	97	−16	23

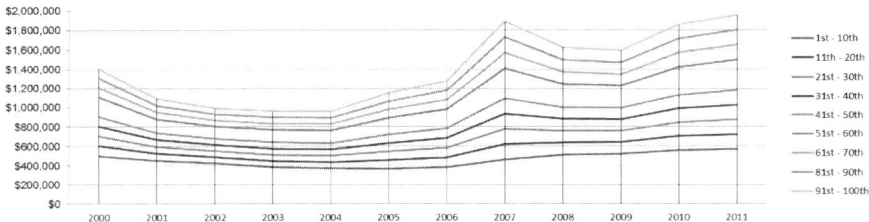

Figure 5. Prices of Private Residential by Decile Over Time.

Between 2004 and 2007, private house prices appreciated in the range of 24% to 97% with the more expensive homes enjoying the largest increase. Table 8 also shows that the properties in the top five deciles were most affected by the subprime crisis.

5. HOUSING AFFORDABILITY

This section presents plots of the computed AaD (d) across household income groups for each category of housing over time. Note that an increase in AaD (d) implies reduced affordability for that particular decile. We also compare our disaggregated measures of housing affordability against those based on the medians alone.

Table 9. Prices of Private Residential by Decile.

Deciles	2000	2001	2002	2003	2004	2005	2006	2007	2008	2009	2010	2011
1st–10th	$500,000	$450,000	$425,000	$380,000	$370,000	$368,000	$380,000	$460,000	$510,000	$520,000	$556,000	$564,800
11th–20th	$601,111	$521,363	$488,267	$444,389	$435,400	$455,347	$480,000	$618,889	$633,732	$638,829	$700,667	$719,822
21st–30th	$702,222	$592,726	$551,533	$508,778	$500,800	$542,693	$580,000	$777,778	$757,464	$757,658	$845,333	$874,844
31st–40th	$803,333	$664,089	$614,800	$573,167	$566,200	$630,040	$680,000	$936,667	$881,196	$876,487	$990,000	$1,029,867
41st–50th	$904,444	$735,452	$678,067	$637,556	$631,600	$717,386	$780,000	$1,095,556	$1,004,928	$995,316	$1,134,667	$1,184,889
51st–60th	$1,005,556	$806,815	$741,333	$701,944	$697,000	$804,733	$880,000	$1,254,444	$1,128,660	$1,114,144	$1,279,333	$1,339,911
61st–70th	$1,106,667	$878,178	$804,600	$766,333	$762,400	$892,079	$980,000	$1,413,333	$1,252,392	$1,232,973	$1,424,000	$1,494,933
71st–80th	$1,207,778	$949,541	$867,867	$830,722	$827,800	$979,426	$1,080,000	$1,572,222	$1,376,124	$1,351,802	$1,568,667	$1,649,956
81st–90th	$1,308,889	$1,020,904	$931,133	$895,111	$893,200	$1,066,772	$1,180,000	$1,731,111	$1,499,856	$1,470,631	$1,713,333	$1,804,978
91st–100th	$1,410,000	$1,092,267	$994,400	$959,500	$958,600	$1,154,119	$1,280,000	$1,890,000	$1,623,587	$1,589,460	$1,858,000	$1,960,000

Table 10. Key Statistics for Prices of Non-Landed Completed Private Residential Properties by Decile.

Deciles	Spread[g] (2001 to 2011)	Percentage change[h] (2001 to 2011)	Average (Over The 11-Year Period)	Maximum (Year)	Minimum (Year)
1st–10th	$64,800	13%	$456,983	$564,800 (2011)	$368,000 (2005)
11th–20th	$118,711	20%	$561,485	$719,822 (2011)	$435,400 (2004)
21st–30th	$172,622	25%	$665,986	$874,844 (2011)	$500,800 (2004)
31st–40th	$226,533	28%	$770,487	$1,029,867 (2011)	$566,200 (2004)
41st–50th	$280,444	31%	$874,988	$1,184,889 (2011)	$631,600 (2004)
51st–60th	$334,356	33%	$979,490	$1,339,911 (2011)	$697,000 (2004)
61st–70th	$388,267	35%	$1,083,991	$1,494,933 (2011)	$762,400 (2004)
71st–80th	$442,178	37%	$1,188,492	$1,649,956 (2011)	$827,800 (2004)
81st–90th	$496,089	38%	$1,292,993	$1,804,978 (2011)	$893,200 (2004)
91st–100th	$550,000	39%	$1,397,494	$1,960,000 (2011)	$958,600 (2004)

[g]Spread = Prices of private residential in 2011 − Prices of private residential in 2000.
[h]Percentage Change = Spread / Prices of private residential in 2000.

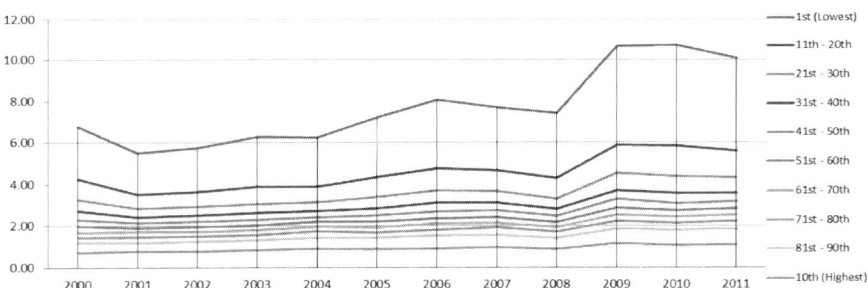

Figure 6. Affordability of New HDB Four-Room Flats by Decile Over Time.

5.1. Affordability of New HDB Flatss

In general, the AaD (d) curves for new four-room HDB flats have moved upward over time, showing that their affordability has declined over the last 11 years. The lower income deciles had higher AaD (d), with the 1st (or lowest) decile having the most significant affordability problem. Figure 6 and Table 11 show that new HDB flats were most affordable in 2000 and

Table 11. Affordability of New HDB Four-Room Flats by Decile, AaD (d).

Deciles	2000	2001	2002	2003	2004	2005	2006	2007	2008	2009	2010	2011
1st (lowest)	6.75	5.51	5.73	6.27	6.23	7.23	8.09	7.70	7.45	10.66	10.74	10.07
11th–20th	4.27	3.52	3.65	3.88	3.89	4.37	4.77	4.67	4.29	5.87	5.85	5.59
21st–30th	3.28	2.86	2.94	3.06	3.16	3.41	3.71	3.68	3.32	4.53	4.40	4.33
31st–40th	2.72	2.43	2.51	2.63	2.72	2.83	3.12	3.13	2.83	3.71	3.58	3.59
41st–50th	2.28	2.15	2.19	2.29	2.41	2.50	2.70	2.74	2.48	3.31	3.10	3.19
51st–60th	1.98	1.89	1.94	2.01	2.19	2.20	2.36	2.41	2.16	2.89	2.75	2.85
61st–70th	1.69	1.69	1.71	1.79	1.95	1.92	2.10	2.14	1.93	2.55	2.44	2.54
71st–80th	1.44	1.46	1.49	1.55	1.73	1.67	1.80	1.91	1.71	2.22	2.14	2.22
81st–90th	1.18	1.19	1.24	1.32	1.42	1.42	1.51	1.55	1.40	1.87	1.79	1.86
10th (highest)	0.72	0.77	0.79	0.83	0.89	0.89	0.92	0.96	0.87	1.15	1.06	1.09

Table 12. Key Statistics for Affordability of New HDB Four-Room Flats by Decile.

Deciles	Percentage Change[i] (2000 to 2011)	Average (Over The 12-Year Period)	Maximum (Year)	Minimum (Year)
1st (lowest)	49%	7.70	10.74 (2010)	5.51 (2001)
11th–20th	31%	4.55	5.87 (2009)	3.52 (2001)
21st–30th	32%	3.56	4.53 (2009)	2.86 (2001)
31st–40th	32%	2.98	3.71 (2009)	2.43 (2001)
41st–50th	40%	2.61	3.31 (2009)	2.15 (2001)
51st–60th	44%	2.30	2.89 (2009)	1.89 (2001)
61st–70th	50%	2.04	2.55 (2009)	1.69 (2001)
71st–80th	54%	1.78	2.22 (2009)	1.44 (2000)
81st–90th	57%	1.48	1.87 (2009)	1.18 (2000)
10th (highest)	53%	0.91	1.15 (2009)	1.15 (2000)

[i]Percentage change = $(AaD\,(d)$ of new HDB flats in 2011 — $AaD\,(d)$ of new HDB flats in 2000)/ $AaD\,(d)$ of new HDB flats in 2000.

2001. This can be attributed to rising annual income levels that peaked at 2001 as well as the relatively benign property market during the same period. Table 12 shows that for many income cohorts, $AaD\,(d)$ peaked in 2009 and declined marginally after that.

From the earlier Table 1, we identify households that are eligible to purchase HDB flats according to the prevailing income ceiling of $8000[3] set by HDB. Table 11 presents the affordability levels of these households using an underscore.[4] There is a clear regressive pattern over time with households in the bottom half of the income distribution experiencing a decline in affordability levels. The lowest income group has seen the most significant erosion in affordability since 2009 as it would take about 10 years of annual income to buy the lowest-priced new flats.

---

[3]From 15 August 2012, the government announced raising the income ceiling from $8,000 to $10,000. This paper still used $8,000 as our data sample is from 2000 to 2011. The adjustment of income ceiling does not affect our analysis.

[4]Suppose employer's CPF contribution rate is 16% of salary up to $5,000, the household income from work including employer's CPF contribution would be $8,800 ($8000 + $5000* 16%). Accordingly annual income ceiling to entitle to buy new HDB flats would be $105,600.

5.2. Affordability of Resale HDB Flats

Figure 7 shows that affordability levels are lower for resale HDB flats than for new HDB flats. The curves in Fig. 7 are also more dispersed than those in the earlier Fig. 6, with greater fluctuations in the affordability indicators. As expected, the 1st decile faces the greatest affordability problem for resale HDB flats. Table 14 shows that $AaD\,(1)$ over the last decade averaged 11.90. In 2011, $AaD\,(1)$ was 16.20 and approximately 71% higher than $AaD\,(1)$ of 9.5 in 2001. Hence, resale HDB flats have become far less affordable over time. The housing affordability of the lowest income decile declined the most in the last decade and would need to be addressed by policymakers.

Comparing Tables 11 and 13, resale flats were almost twice (about 1.7 times) as unaffordable as new flats over the last decade. Hence, there would be a continuing reliance on the state to provide affordable public housing and housing grants to support lower income groups seeking to own a home.

5.3. Affordability of Private Residential Properties

The computed $AaD\,(d)$ ratios for private residential properties are much higher than those of new and resale HDB flats. From Tables 13 and 15, the $AaD\,(d)$ of private property in 2011 is at least twice that of resale HDB flats for the majority of income deciles. However, housing affordability for private housing has generally improved from 2000 to 2011; other than

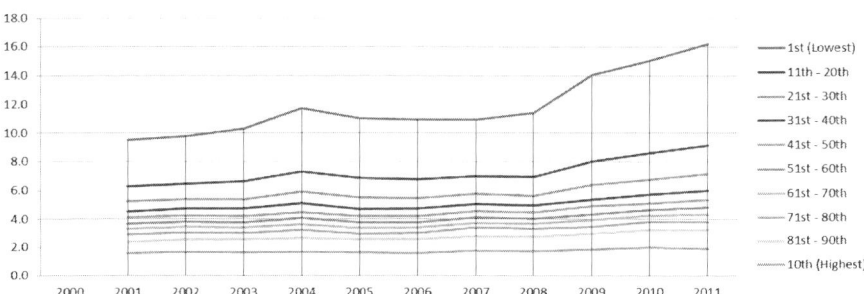

Figure 7. Affordability of Resale HDB Four-Room Flats by Decile Over Time.

Table 13. Affordability of Resale HDB Flats by Decile, AaD (d).

Deciles	2000	2001	2002	2003	2004	2005	2006	2007	2008	2009	2010	2011
1st (lowest)	—	9.50	9.76	10.31	11.72	11.02	10.93	10.93	11.42	14.05	15.04	16.20
11th–20th	—	6.29	6.48	6.62	7.31	6.88	6.75	7.02	6.97	8.05	8.62	9.15
21st–30th	—	5.24	5.40	5.38	5.92	5.53	5.46	5.77	5.65	6.41	6.78	7.18
31st–40th	—	4.55	4.74	4.74	5.11	4.70	4.76	5.08	4.99	5.39	5.72	6.01
41st–50th	—	4.11	4.25	4.20	4.51	4.24	4.23	4.59	4.51	4.92	5.13	5.39
51st–60th	—	3.68	3.84	3.76	4.10	3.80	3.79	4.13	4.02	4.37	4.68	4.86
61st–70th	—	3.34	3.45	3.41	3.65	3.36	3.43	3.74	3.68	3.93	4.24	4.36
71st–80th	—	2.91	3.04	2.99	3.23	2.97	3.01	3.40	3.31	3.48	3.81	3.83
81st–90th	—	2.40	2.58	2.57	2.65	2.55	2.56	2.80	2.76	2.96	3.24	3.24
10th (highest)	—	1.57	1.66	1.64	1.66	1.60	1.58	1.76	1.73	1.85	1.96	1.91

Table 14. Key Statistics for Affordability of Resale HDB Four-Room Flats by Decile.

Deciles	Percentage change[j] (2001 to 2011)	Average (Over The 11-Year Period)	Maximum (Year)	Minimum (Year)
1st (lowest)	70%	11.90	16.20(2011)	9.50(2001)
11th–20th	46%	7.29	9.15(2011)	6.29(2001)
21st–30th	37%	5.88	7.18(2011)	5.24(2001)
31st–40th	32%	5.07	6.01(2011)	4.55(2001)
41st–50th	31%	4.55	5.39(2011)	4.11(2001)
51st–60th	32%	4.09	4.86(2011)	3.68(2001)
61st–70th	31%	3.69	4.36(2011)	3.34(2001)
71st–80th	32%	3.27	3.83(2011)	2.91(2001)
81st–90th	35%	2.76	3.24(2011)	2.40(2001)
10th (highest)	21%	1.72	1.96(2010)	1.57(2001)

[j]Percentage change = $(AaD\,(d)$ of resale HDB flats in 2011 $-$ $AaD\,(d)$ of resale HDB flats in 2001)/ $AaD\,(d)$ of resale HDB flats in 2001.

the lowest income decile, the AaD ratios for the other deciles dropped by about 14% to 20%. We attribute this to the fact that household incomes have increased faster relative to private house prices than to public house prices over the sample period.

5.4. The Significance of a Disaggregated Approach

We compare the results of our disaggregated approach to those obtained by looking only at the median levels. Our data allows us to compute the medians for the private housing sector, which are presented in Table 17. Annual affordability ratios of median private residential price to the median annual household income are shown in Table 17. The ratios move within a tighter band and understate the difficulty of housing affordability for the lower income deciles. From our results above in Table 16, the lowest income decile had affordability ratios ranging from 24.4 to 31.84 over the last decade.

Table 15. Affordability of Private Residential Decile.

Deciles	2000	2001	2002	2003	2004	2005	2006	2007	2008	2009	2010	2011
1st–10th	30.15	28.17	27.98	25.89	25.03	24.40	25.17	29.02	30.38	31.84	30.95	29.77
11th–20th	22.35	19.10	18.66	17.11	16.50	16.81	17.35	21.33	19.56	19.75	19.86	19.13
21st–30th	19.60	16.23	15.61	14.21	13.97	14.51	15.19	19.18	16.48	16.67	16.94	16.49
31st–40th	18.18	14.31	13.77	12.75	12.46	13.06	14.03	18.01	14.97	14.67	15.23	14.81
41st–50th	16.73	13.10	12.36	11.46	11.32	12.30	13.08	17.04	13.83	13.87	14.32	14.04
51st–60th	15.80	11.84	11.19	10.38	10.55	11.43	12.17	15.93	12.55	12.69	13.60	13.24
61st–70th	14.51	10.84	10.06	9.50	9.58	10.42	11.37	14.86	11.65	11.68	12.75	12.33
71st–80th	13.23	9.51	8.89	8.41	8.61	9.45	10.22	13.82	10.60	10.53	11.77	11.17
81st–90th	11.53	7.91	7.54	7.26	7.19	8.31	8.90	11.65	8.92	9.13	10.24	9.70
91st–100th	7.37	5.21	4.88	4.66	4.57	5.32	5.58	7.45	5.64	5.78	6.33	5.86

Table 16. Key Statistics for Affordability of Private Residential Property by Decile.

Deciles	Percentage Change[k] (2000 to 2011)	Average (Over The 12-Year Period)	Maximum (Year)	Minimum (Year)
1st–10th	−1%	28.23	31.84 (2009)	24.40 (2005)
11th–20th	−14%	18.96	22.35 (2000)	16.50 (2004)
21st–30th	−16%	16.26	19.60 (2000)	13.97 (2004)
31st–40th	−19%	14.69	18.18 (2000)	12.46 (2004)
41st–50th	−16%	13.62	17.04 (2007)	11.32 (2004)
51st–60th	−16%	12.61	15.93 (2007)	10.38 (2003)
61st–70th	−15%	11.63	14.86 (2007)	9.50 (2003)
71st–80th	−16%	10.52	13.82 (2007)	8.41 (2003)
81st–90th	−16%	9.02	11.65 (2007)	7.19 (2004)
91st–100th	−20%	5.72	7.45 (2007)	4.57 (2004)

[k] Percentage change = $(AaD(d)$ of private residential property in 2011 − $AaD(d)$ of private residential property in 2000) / $AaD(d)$ of private residential property in 2000.

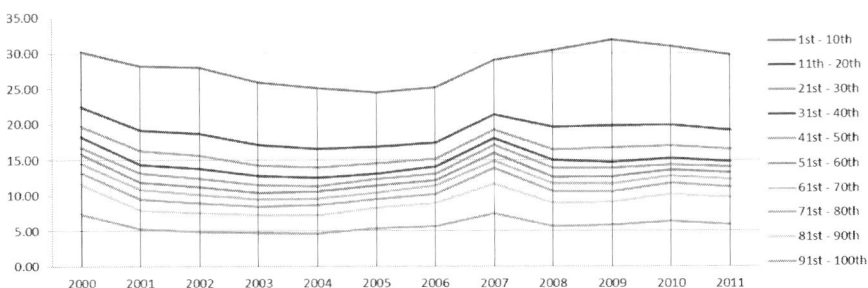

Figure 8. Affordability of Private Residential Properties by Decile Over Time.

As we are unable to get the medians for HDB prices, we compare our results for the HDB sector with those obtained in Phang (2009). These are reproduced in Table 18 and are based on the estimated median house price to median household income ratio.

Compared with the earlier Table 11, the aggregated approach understates the housing affordability problem for households of lower income.

Table 17. Affordability of Private Residential Properties — Aggregated Approach.

Year	2000	2001	2002	2003	2004	2005	2006	2007	2008	2009	2010	2011
Annual Median Household Income	$52,776	$56,592	$55,080	$55,344	$54,624	$57,972	$59,424	$64,344	$73,200	$72,072	$76,104	$84,444
Non-landed Non central Private Residential Prices	$772,000	$650,000	$626,400	$594,880	$605,000	$620,000	$660,000	$802,000	$820,000	$825,000	$942,000	$980,000
Ratio of Median House Price to Annual Household Income	14.63	11.49	11.37	10.75	11.08	10.69	11.11	12.46	11.20	11.45	12.38	11.61

Table 18. Affordability of New HDB Flats — Aggregated Approach.

Year	Ratio of Median House Price to Annual Median Household Income	Year-on-Year Percentage Change
1999	4.3	—
2000	4.0	−7%
2001	3.8	−5%
2002	3.8	0%
2003	3.9	3%
2004	4.0	3%
2005	4.1	2%
2006	4.5	10%
2007	4.1	−9%
2008	4.2	2%

AaD (1) was between 5.51 and 10.74 for the lowest income decile in the past decade. It means that the situation of median income moving in tandem with median prices does not necessarily mean affordable house prices, especially for the 1st decile income households.

6. CONCLUSION

This paper advocates using a disaggregated approach to measure the housing affordability levels of households across the entire income distribution. We compute affordability ratios for each income decile cohort for new and resale HDB flats as well as suburban private housing. Based on our analysis, housing prices have outstripped household incomes, particularly for households in the lower half of the income distribution. Hence, housing affordability has generally deteriorated over the past decade. New HDB flats were least affordable in 2009 for the majority of household income deciles except for the lowest income decile who fared worst in 2010. Resale HDB flats were least affordable in 2011 and with its upward trajectory, affordability levels would continue to be under pressure. For non-landed and completed private residential housing in the mass market, affordability ratios were relatively flat from 2000 to 2011 which suggests that housing affordability for private housing in Singapore has improved for the past decade. This is in relative terms: public housing has appreciated faster than private housing over our sample period compared to household incomes.

There is a regressive affordability pattern among the different income groups. The lowest income decile faced the greatest challenges, as households in this cohort saw a worsening of their affordability problem over time. Such a pattern would be masked using traditional measures that focus only on medians or averages. Hence, use of a disaggregated approach provides a more nuanced view than conventional measures of affordability. Based on our data, median measures would probably understate the housing affordability problem in Singapore, especially for the lower income households. By taking into account the whole distribution of incomes and house prices, a disaggregated approach is more useful for policy makers to identify disadvantaged groups and to target policies toward those with the greatest challenges.

7. COMMENTS ON PRESENTATION BY SPEAKER

Discussant: Mr Christopher Gee

Research Fellow, Institute of Public Policy

7.1. Housing and Inequality: Short–Medium Term Imbalances

Prof. Lum's presentation provides strong evidence of the relationship between property prices and the economy. From various property indices and periods of negative real economic growth — the Asian Financial Crisis (AFC) 1998, the post-dotcom bust/Iraq war recession, severe acute respiratory syndrome (SARS) and the Global Financial Crisis (GFC) in 2008/2009 — we see that property prices already started to fall before the negative real gross domestic product (GDP) growth period. This is pretty normal — in the US, property prices started to fall in 2007, almost a year and a half ahead of the GFC, as there were lags in the economic data and the broader economy has more momentum than specific asset markets.

There may therefore be periods in the market when changes in household income lag behind house price changes, whilst across the household income distribution, specific labor micro-market dynamics may cause disparities and divergences in apparent housing affordability measures in the short-to-medium run.

7.2. A Perspective on Housing Affordability

Housing affordability can be considered from two angles: either by reference to price-to-income ratios or to debt service ratios. Prof. Lum mentioned that in Singapore, most studies tend to focus on debt service ratios given the additional dimension introduced by the use of CPF savings for housing purchases. Debt service ratios consider affordability from the perspective of repaying a mortgage. In Singapore, there is a unique aspect to this capability — the rapid accumulation of housing equity by households who are already on the property ladder, aided by the subsidies and grants for eligible home buyers from the (HDB), and the rise in HDB resale values. Previous work regarding HDB housing equity accumulation show that it is at this point where households in the 75–85th percentile of income (living in four- or five-bedroom HDB flats) upgrade to private housing. That is, if they were able to sell the HDB flat and use the equity in their HDB flat as the down payment on a private property, they needed to do it as soon as possible, in order to make it up the next significant step on the housing ladder.

Another related issue is the proper matching of the expectations of HDB applicants with the supply of flats by the HDB. Given the additional implicit subsidy provided by the HDB to first-time flat-buyers beyond the initial grants offered to eligible buyers (i.e., house price appreciation during the period of ownership accrues to the HDB apartment owner), applicants have the greatest incentive to maximize this implicit subsidy by applying for the largest and most attractive flat from a resale perspective as possible (even though it may be beyond their requirements in the next five to six years). Notions of affordability have to be calibrated with the realistic expectations of the house buyer. It may not be realistic for a young couple with a household income at the 21–30th percentile to expect to find a four- or five-bedroom apartment in a mature HDB township like Clementi (which costs around $430,000) affordable.

7.3. Housing Supply and Demand Considerations

Figure 9 shows the completed HDB residential units those under construction from financial years (FYs) 2002 to 2011. Many of us will recall that in the early 2000s, the HDB was left with a lot of unsold inventory, and shifted

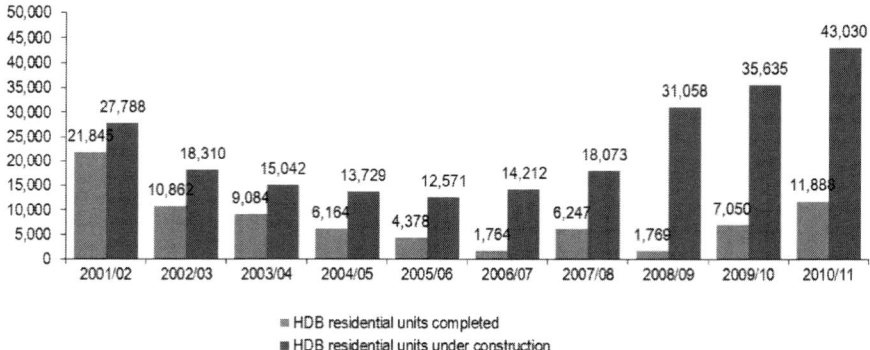

Figure 9. HDB Residential Units Under Construction and Completed.
Source: HDB Annual reports from FY01/02 to FY10/11.

to a Build-to-Order (BTO) supply model. This came on the back of a major structural change in the economy in the context of the post-dotcom bust, SARS and significant changes to maximum CPF withdrawals for housing as a result of the recommendations of the Economic Review Committee (ERC). Unsurprisingly, completions in the six-year period from FY03/04 to FY09/10 averaged only 4600 units a year. By way of reference, household formation rate in Singapore is 20,000–25,000 each year, where at least 75% of new households would seek public housing. Just from resident household formation then, we have a backlog of demand for about 60,000 homes. On top of this, Singapore's population experienced a significant increase from 2005 onwards. With half a million additional residents in Singapore (many of whom are foreigners, newcomers which needed to be housed as well), the rental market was boosted and home resale prices rose (either through investment demand yields or from eligible Permanent Residents buying for personal consumption). Even with the 20,000–25,000 new HDB flats in the next three or four years, we are still only catching up with the backlog of demand over the past five–six years, much less with new household formations each year.

7.4. Correct Measurement of House Price Changes

The NUS SRPI is a transactions-based index put together by the NUS Department of Real Estate (DRE) to complement and improve the official private residential price indices compiled by the URA. Monthly changes are methodologically different from the URA price index, wherein the NUS SPRI charts monthly changes does not incorporate primary market transactions. New sale or primary market transactions are those between developer and house buyer, most often pre-completion. These primary sales therefore represent a futures market for housing, in that it cannot satisfy a current consumption need. More investment demand is present in the futures market as well. A normal futures market is typically in contango (meaning the futures price is generally higher than the spot market). Thus, an aggregated price index that incorporates both primary as well as resale transactions will typically have an upward bias, at least in a normal market. In 2011, primary market transactions outweighed resale transactions by a 55:45 ratio. In Hong Kong, by comparison, the typical primary market to secondary market transaction ratio is 1:3.

The ratio of market transaction is important because we use these indicators as a reference point for the inflation — Consumer Price Index (CPI) expectations are based on the movement of these figures and self-reinforcing expectations may also be built in. Use of the appropriate measures for house price changes — in terms of providing accurate and reliable indication of the state and direction of the market — is necessary for the market participants and the policymakers to act appropriately.

7.5. Housing: A Force Against Inequality in Singapore, Historically and Now

Singapore's public housing system has been a roaring success. If one looks at home ownership rates — the amount of housing equity for households at all percentiles compared with other markets — the country has been very effective in making sure of near-universal housing for those who need help the most. Society has benefitted from positive externalities that arise from this high rate of home ownership, such as lower crime rates, better schools, and better public services. I would argue that the public housing system is one of the most powerful forces countering inequality in Singapore. If one had to do a Gini co-efficient for just the housing sector, comparing housing arrangements by income distribution of the population (e.g., the way in which the bottom third are housed in terms of quality

162 Inequality in Singapore

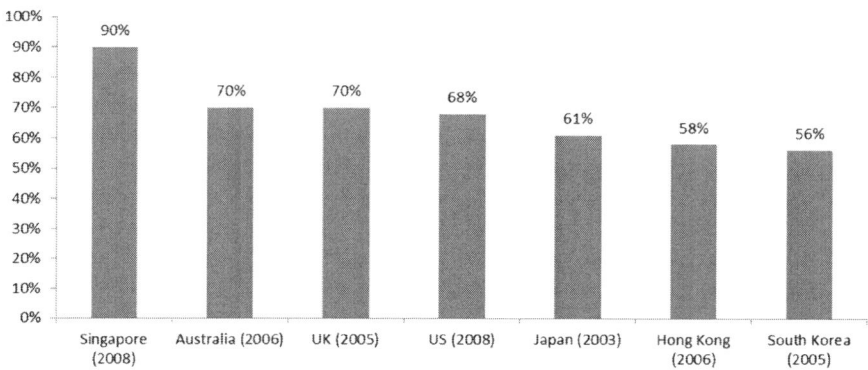

Figure 10. Home Ownership Rates (Selected Countries).

Sources: Singapore Department of Statistics, 2008; Australia Bureau of Statistics, Yearbook Australia 2006); United Kingdom Communities and Local Government data, 2005; US Census Bureau, 2008; Japan Statistical Yearbook, 2009; Hong Kong Housing Authority, 2006; National Statistics Office, South Korea, 2005.

and their housing rights/equity) — Singapore would compare well with other countries with superior Gini co-efficients of income such as Sweden. If you look at some of the transfers from government to households, it has been quite substantial — just the government grant to HDB (basically offsetting the HDB's operating deficits) over the last 11 years, amounts to $10.7 billion, or equivalent to about S$1000 each year per HDB household. And this does not include the indirect benefit to some households of subsidized housing loans. Moreover, HDB does not require the repayment of grants that it has given, if HDB flats are sold at a profit.

The success of the system has made homeowners for 90% of households here (Figure 10), but the consequences of this success may result in high expectations about future returns from this asset class, in particular if we confront the age structure of the population. The three charts in Figure 11 show the resident population pyramid in 2005, compared with IPS' projections of the resident population, under conditions of a 1.24 Total Fertility Rate (TFR) with no in-migration.

7.6. Housing: The Intergenerational Transfer That is Looming

The dynamics that an aging population will likely pose on the housing sector are very profound. We are likely to witness a very substantial

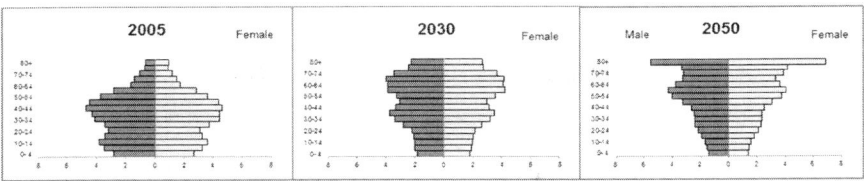

Figure 11. Singapore's Ageing Population.

Source: Singapore Department of Statistics for 2005, IPS projections for 2030 and 2050 on resident population with TFR = 1.24 and no in-migration.

intergenerational transfer of housing equity in the next two to three decades. Can a predominantly market-based valuation mechanism allow this transfer to be made equitably across the generations, given the complexities and the intertwining of the housing finance system with retirement adequacy? We may move to a situation where the government may need to more effectively assist (and perhaps even make additional transfers to) retirees to monetize their properties; the next 40 years will coincide with large portions of Singapore's public housing stock moving below 50 years of remaining land lease. It will also mean the reversal of funds-flows into the system, with greater withdrawals from the upper ends of the property ladder than the inputs from younger generation first time home buyers. The manner in which this intergenerational transfer is handled will likely have exceedingly significant implications on the social and political compact in Singapore.

REFERENCES

Abeysinghe, T and JY Gu (2011). Lifetime income and housing affordability in Singapore. *Urban Studies*, 48(9), 1875–1891.

Burke, T (2003). Housing affordability. Paper presented at the *AHURI workshop of the Swinburne Monash AHURI centre*, 13 November. Melbourne, Australia: Swinburne University of Technology.

Chan, F (2009). Are private homes getting out of reach? *The Straits Times*, A36, 19 September. global.factiva.com

Demographia International (2008). 4th Annual Demographia International Housing Affordability Survey. http://demographia.com/dhi2008.pdf.

DTZ (2010). Mass market housing affordability for Singapore Q1 2010. DTZ Research, DTZ Insight. Available at http://www.dtz.com/Singapore.

Gan, H and RJ Hill (2009). Measuring housing affordability: Looking beyond the median. *Journal of Housing Economics*, 18(2), 115–125.

Hancock, KE (1993). Can pay? Won't pay? or economic principles of affordability. *Urban Studies*, 30(1), 127–145.

Kamath, R (1988). The measurement of housing affordability. *Real Estate Issues*, Fall/Winter, 26–33.

Kazakevitch, G and L Borrowman (2009). Housing affordability: Proper measurement for informed policy making. Paper presented at the *Australian Conference of Economists*, 28 September. Adelaide, Australia.

Lum, SK (1996). The Singapore private property market-price trends and affordability. Paper presented at the *NUS Inter-Faculty Conference on The Singapore Dream: Private Property, Social Expectations and Public Policy*, 6 September. Singapore: National University of Singapore.

Mah, BT (2009). Parliamentary Speech by Minister for National Development at Committee of Supply Debate, Singapore, 6 February.

Ndubueze, O (2007). Measuring housing affordability: A composite approach. Paper presented at the *ENHR 2007 International Conference "Sustainable Urban Areas"*, 25–28 June. Rotterdam.

Ong, SE (2000). Housing affordability and upward mobility from public to private housing in Singapore. *International Real Estate Review*, 3(1), 49–64.

Phang, SY (2009). Affordable homeownership policy: Implications for housing markets. SMU Economics & Statistics working paper 14-2009, Singapore Management University, The School of Economics.

Robinson, M, GM Scobbie and B Hallinan (2006). Affordability of housing: concepts, measurements and evidence. NZTworking paper 06/03, New Zealand Treasury, New Zealand.

Singapore Department of Statistics (n. d.). Household income from work. http://www.singstat.gov.sg/stats/themes/people/hhldincome.

Urban Redevelopment Authority, Singapore (n. d.). Real estate information system (REALIS). http://spring.ura.gov.sg.

Yuen, B, L Kwee and Y Tu (2006). Housing affordability in Singapore: can we move from public to private housing? *Urban Policy and Research*, 24(2), 253–270.

ABOUT THE SPEAKERS

Paul CHEUNG, a national of Singapore, is Professor of Social Policy and Analytics at the National University of Singapore. He returned to Singapore in 2013 after serving nine years as the Director of the United Nations Statistics Division (UNSD) at the United Nations Headquarters in New York (2004–2012). At the UN, he facilitated the development of the global statistical system and coordinated the work of the United Nations Statistical Commission. In 2011, his initiative of establishing an inter-governmental platform to address critical issues on Global Geospatial Information Management (UN-GGIM) was endorsed by the UN. Prior to his appointment at the UN, he served as Chief Statistician of the Government of Singapore (1991–2004). He was awarded the Public Administration Medal (Gold) by the Singapore Government and the Royal Order of Sahametrei (Grand Officer) by the Government of Cambodia. He received his PhD from the University of Michigan and Dr.h.c. from National University of Mongolia.

HUI Weng Tat is Associate Professor at the Lee Kuan Yew School of Public Policy (LKY School). He specializes in the impact of globalization on labour markets, economic issues of migration, education, ageing and retirement, income inequality and labour market policies in Singapore. He has also taught in the Department of Economics at the National University of Singapore (NUS) before joining the LKY School at NUS in 2004. He has published in international labour and public economics journals, and co-edited and contributed to the book *Singapore Economy in the 21st Century: Issues and Strategies (McGraw Hill)*. He has acted as a consultant to the Ministry of Manpower, the International Labour Organization and was the Associate Research Fellow of the then Singapore Institute of Labour

Studies from 1991–1994. He also served as a resource person to the National Wages Council and was a member of the Economic Review Sub-Committee Workgroup on Wages, the Institute of Policy Studies Economic Restructuring Working Group, the Economic Strategies Committee Workgroup on Workforce Skills and Low Wage Workers and REACH's Policy Study Workgroup on Manpower Issues. He has held various administrative appointments which include Deputy Director of the Public Policy Programme (1997–1998), Deputy and Acting Head of the Department of Economics (1998–2000), Vice Dean (Research & Graduate Studies) of the NUS Faculty of Arts and Social Sciences (2000–2003) and Vice Dean (Academic Affairs) of the LKY School (2004–2008). At the LKY School, he teaches graduate courses on Economics and Public Policy, Public Policy Research and Evaluation, and Labour Market Policy Issues.

LUM Sau Kim is the Director of Graduate Programs at the Department of Real Estate, School of Design and Environment, National University of Singapore (NUS). She also heads the NUS Singapore Residential Price Index (SRPI) project. Sau Kim obtained her PhD. in Business Administration, co-majoring in Finance and Real Estate, from the Haas Business School at UC Berkeley. A former Asean, Public Service Commission and British Commonwealth scholar, she is the recipient of several Faculty and University Teaching Excellence awards. She is also a Post-Doctoral Scholar honoree of the Weimer School of Advanced Studies in Real Estate and Land Economics. Since 1999, Sau Kim has consulted for various public sector agencies and private corporations. In 2013, she chaired the expert sessions on housing for the "Our Singapore Conversation" dialogue. Her research interests are in the areas of urban economics, housing policy and index construction.

Irene Y.H. NG is an Associate Professor of Social Work at the National University of Singapore and Executive Editor of Asia Pacific Journal of Social Work and Development. She holds a joint Ph.D. in Social Work and Economics from the University of Michigan. Her research areas include poverty and inequality, intergenerational mobility, youth crime, and social welfare policy. She is Principal Investigator of an evaluation of a national Work Support programme and Co-Principal Investigator of National Youth Surveys 2010 and 2013. She has served in committees in the National Youth

Council, the Chinese Development Assistance Council, and the Family Research Network. Her teaching areas include poverty, policy, research, youth work, and programme planning.

PHUA Kai Hong holds a tenured appointment at the Lee Kuan Yew School of Public Policy and teaches health and social policy, health care management, health economics and global health at the National University of Singapore (NUS). He was previously Associate Professor and Head, Health Services Research at the Faculty of Medicine, NUS and was also an Adjunct Senior Fellow at the Institute of Policy Studies, Singapore. He graduated with honours *cum laude* from Harvard University and received graduate degrees from the Harvard School of Public Health (Master's in Health Services Administration & Population Sciences) and the London School of Economics & Political Science (PhD in Health Economics). He has produced numerous papers in the field of health policy and management, including the history of health services, population ageing and care of the elderly, health economics and financing, comparative health policy and health sector reforms in the Asia-Pacific region.

He is a founding member of the Asian Health Systems Reform Network (DRAGONET), Chairman of the Executive Board of the Asia-Pacific Health Economics Network (APHEN), and past Chair of the Asia-Pacific Medical Devices and Diagnostics Council, International Society for Pharmacoeconomics and Outcomes Research (ISPOR). He was appointed to many national advisory committees on health-related issues in Singapore and is a past Vice-Chairman of the Singapore Red Cross. He has undertaken healthcare consulting assignments for international organizations including the Asian Development Bank, United Nations Economic and Social Commission for the Asia-Pacific, World Bank, World Health Organization, and ministries of health throughout Asia-Pacific and the Middle East. He has also served as Chairman, Technical Advisory Group on Health Sector Development of the WHO Western Pacific Regional Office, and moderator of several WHO regional meetings on health systems.

SHANDRE Thangavelu is an active Researcher on human capital development, technology transfer, foreign direct investment, trade, government infrastructure investment, productivity and economic growth. He has written extensively in technology transfer and economic growth and has published his research in major international journals. His recent publications are in Journal of Development Economics, Empirical Economics, Applied Economics, World Economy, and Journal of Economic Studies. Recently, he was attached as the Head of the Economics Unit, Ministry of Manpower (MOM), under the Economist Service to Ministry of Trade and Industry and Ministry of Manpower. He has also worked on several international projects commissioned by Asian Productivity Organization (APO) on the measurement of aggregate productivity for the Singapore economy and the World Bank project on structural changes and skill-mismatch. Currently, he is working as a Consultant and Country Expert on the Expert Group EFTA Study Phase II that comprises experts from ASEAN, China, Korea and Japan. He is also assisting as a Consultant (Head of Economics Unit) to MOM.

Associate Professor Shandre was the Director of SCAPE (Singapore Centre for Applied and Policy Economics) at the Department of Economics, Faculty of Arts and Social Sciences, National University of Singapore. He was also the Assistant Dean at the Faculty of Arts and Social Sciences from January 2004 to May 2006. Recently, he was appointed as the Managing Editor for Asian Economic Journal (AEJ). He is also a Senior Research Fellow at Leverhulme Centre for Research on Globalisation and Economic Policy (GEP), University of Nottingham; and Faculty Associate (Research) at Institute of Policy Studies at Lee Kuan Yew School of Public Policy, National University of Singapore. He obtained his graduate degrees from Queen's University, Canada. Currently, Associate Professor Shandre is the Regional Director (SEA) at Institute of International Trade, University of Adelaide, Australia.

TAN Khee Giap is Associate Professor at the Lee Kuan Yew School of Public Policy. He is also Chair of Singapore National Committee for Pacific Economic Cooperation.

Upon graduating with a PhD from University of East Anglia, England, UK in 1987, he joined the banking sector as a treasury manager and served as secretary to the Assets and Liabilities Committee for three years, there after he taught at the Department of Economics and Statistics, National University of Singapore (NUS), 1990–1993. Professor Tan joined Nanyang

Technological University in 1993 and was Associate Dean, Graduate Studies Office, 2007–2009. He is now the Co-Director of Asia Competitiveness Institute at Lee Kuan Yew School of Public Policy, NUS.

Professor Tan has consulted extensively with the various government ministries, statutory boards and government-linked companies of Singapore government on policies concerning financial, fiscal, trade, tourism, public housing, labor, telecommunication, tourism, liveable cities, creative industry, media, community development, airport and seaport activities. He has also served as a consultant to international agencies such as the Asian Development Bank, Asian Development Bank Institute, United Nations Industrial Development Group, World Gold Council, ASEAN Secretariat, Central Policy Unit of Hong Kong, Kerzner International, Las Vegas Sands, and other international financial institutions and multinational corporations.

Professor Tan has widely published in international refereed journals such as Applied Economics (United Kingdom), ASEAN Economic Bulletin (Singapore), Asian Economic Papers (United States), Competitiveness Review (USA), Competitiveness Review: An International Business Journal incorporating Journal of Global Competitiveness, (United Kingdom), International Journal of Business Competition and Growth (United Kingdom), International Journal of Chinese Culture and Business Management (United Kingdom), International Journal of Economics and Business Research (United Kingdom), International Journal of Indian Culture and Business Management (United Kingdom), Journal of Centrum Cathedra The Business and Economics Research Journal (Peru), Journal of International Commerce, Economics and Policy, Journal of Southeast Asian Economies (Singapore), Review of Pacific Basin Financial Markets and Policies (United States), and World Review of Science, Technology and Sustainable Development (Switzerland). His current research interests include econometric forecasting, financial reforms and liberalization of ASEAN 10 + 5 Economies, Global Liveable Cities Index and competitiveness analysis on 31 provinces in China, 35 states in India and Asean-10 economies.

ABOUT THE DISCUSSANTS

CHAN Beng Seng was the Divisional Director overseeing the Income Security Policy Division in the Ministry of Manpower at the time of the discussion. He was responsible for CPF policies, measures to uplifting of low-wage workers, and raising compliance with employment laws. Beng Seng has more than 15 years of experience in the civil service, and has served in the Ministry of Transport, the Ministry of Trade and Industry and the then-Ministry of Community Development, Youth and Sports and other government agencies. He currently serves as the Deputy Chief Executive of the People's Association. Beng Seng read economics at the London School of Economics and holds an MBA from the Harvard Business School.

Christopher GEE is a Research Fellow at the Institute of Policy Studies. He has worked in investment banking, analyzing the real estate sector (developers and REITs) in various markets in the Asia region for the past eleven years. He was rated the top Singapore analyst in the Institutional Investor surveys from 2005 to 2010. He was the Head of Asia Real Estate Equities Research for J.P. Morgan from end 2006 to early 2012. Mr Gee joined J.P. Morgan in Singapore in August 2002 as Head of Equities Research from ING Financial Markets, where he was the head of equities research for Singapore and Malaysia from 2000. Prior to relocating to Singapore in 2000, he was based in Kuala Lumpur as the head of equities research and an investment analyst at ING Barings in Malaysia covering the real estate, infrastructure, and insurance sectors (amongst others). He holds the CFA charter and trained as a chartered accountant with Price Waterhouse in London in early 1990s. He is now working in the Demography and Family cluster at the Institute of Policy Studies.

LIM Sia Hoe started her career with Singapore Organisation of Seamen (SOS), an affiliated union to NTUC as Industrial Relations Officer (Welfare) in 1982 after graduating in Economics from the University of Malaya. Her 12 years of union work in providing welfare support to seafarers and their families; includes setting up of SeaCare Cooperative Ltd for seamen in 1994.

From 1995 to 2005, she spent ten years of her career in Orchid Country Club from being a Social & Recreation/Membership Manager to Senior Manager (Operations). She was responsible for day-to-day operations and management of the Club and her key contributions were revamping the whole membership system and scheme, organize an Asian Professional Golf Championship — Nokia Open, which brought in international golf professionals to Orchid Country Club and conceptualize and oversee the development of the Recreation complex.

In 2005, Ms Lim made a choice to step outside of the safety of working/living on auto-pilot and do something that engages her heart. She joined NTUC Eldercare. She started off with an all-conquering eagerness to do more, better and faster, only to realise the immense difficulty of the tasks and challenges ahead. The economics do not add up; the need for care and support is never-ending. Yet cost is always a barrier, community support services are fragmented and the glamour for this sector is almost non-existent.

In the last five years, she has re-defined the service model of day-care centres and develop a systematic engagement programme with health and wellness elements in the care plans for senior clients, offer a new take to the service delivery model to home help and home nursing services and tapping on the potential assets in domestic helpers in providing better care to elderly through structured training and support. The service delivery model however is shape by the set of boundaries that was defined by the grant-makers and donors.

TAN Ern Ser is Associate Professor, Department of Sociology, and Head, Social Lab, Institute of Policy Studies, at the National University of Singapore. He received his PhD in Sociology from Cornell University, USA.

Dr Tan has written on social stratification, welfare policy, ethnic relations, and politics and democracy. He is author of "Does Class Matter? Social Stratification and Orientations in Singapore" (2004). He completed a study on social stratification in Singapore in 2011, a sequel to his 2001 study on the same subject. He is co-principal investigator of Asian Barometer-Singapore (with Dr Gillian Koh), as well as World Values Survey-Singapore (with UniSIM researchers).

Dr Tan has served as principal consultant to the National Orientations of Singaporeans (NOS) survey series I-IV, and a consultant to the National Survey of Senior Citizens 2005 and 2011, the Learning Needs of Senior Citizens 2008, as well as REACH (Reaching Everyone for Active Citizenry@ Home). He is also a Research Adviser to the Ministry of Social and Family Development and a member of the HDB (Housing Development Board) Research Advisory Panel. He was appointed a Justice of Peace in 2013.

WONG Su-Yen is a Senior Partner and Chairman, Singapore for Marsh & McLennan Companies. She is concurrently Senior Advisor to Mercer and Oliver Wyman.

She brings over 20 years' experience in business strategy, operations redesign, strategic talent development, and organization transformation. She has advised clients across Asia since 1995, and was previously based in the United States, Thailand, Korea, and Hong Kong. She has worked with leading organizations across North America and Asia in a broad range of industries including high-tech, financial services, oil and gas, aerospace, retail/consumer, and the public sector.

Previously she was Managing Director for Mercer in ASEAN where she was responsible for driving results across Talent, Health, Retirement, and Investments in Southeast Asia. Prior to Mercer, she was a Director and the Asia Managing Partner for the Communications, Information & Entertainment practice at Oliver Wyman. Su-Yen is a highly regarded speaker and facilitator at conferences in Asia. She has published articles and is often quoted in print and broadcast media, including CNBC, Channel News Asia, The Wall Street Journal, and Bloomberg. She brings deep knowledge of human capital issues, and led the study of Progressive Labour Practices to Enhance the Competitiveness of ASEAN, on behalf of the ASEAN Secretariat's Ad-Hoc Working Group on Progressive Labour Practices and the Ministry of Manpower, Singapore. She also co-led the Mercer team that advised the Committee to Review Ministerial Salaries in Singapore. In 2012, she was named to The Agenda Compensation 100: Top Board Candidates with Pay Setting Skills.

Su-Yen is Independent Director, Chairman of the Nominating Committee, and a member of the Remuneration Committee, Nera Telecommunications. She is also a Director and member of the Remuneration Committee, National Kidney Foundation. She is an active member of the Singapore Institute of Directors, and the Young Presidents' Organization. She holds a B.A. (summa cum laude) in music and computer science from Linfield College and an M.B.A. from the University of North Carolina at Chapel Hill.

YEOH Lam Keong is an Adjunct Senior Research Fellow at the Institute of Policy Studies. Mr Yeoh had a long and distinguished career in international finance and fund management. He worked as a senior economist and strategist at the Government of Singapore Investment Corporation for 26 years where he was Director of Economics and Strategy and Chief Economist from October 2000 to June 2011. He brings with him a wealth of experience in the areas of global economic analysis and investment research management, as well as global currency/asset allocation strategy.

Mr Yeoh is also a prominent economist in Singapore and is heavily involved in public policy research. He is an active public policy commentator and analyst and has been an advisor to a number of research institutes in Singapore including the Singapore Centre for Applied Policy Economics (SCAPE) at the National University of Singapore (NUS), the Singapore Management University (SMU) faculty of economics, and the government feedback unit REACH. He is an Adjunct Senior Fellow at the Institute of Policy Studies and a Fellow of the Civil Service College.

Mr Yeoh graduated with a BSc (Econs) and MSc (Econs) from the London School of Economics and Political Science. He is married with two children.

INDEX

absolute social mobility, 43
Adam Smith, 126
Additional CPF Housing Grant (AHG), 141
Activities of Daily Living (ADL), 112, 115, 123, 129, 130
affordability index for public housing, 19
ageing labor force, 4, 78, 79
ageing population, 7, 8, 10, 42, 56, 70, 81, 163
Agency for Integrated Care (AIC), 113, 125, 131
Amartya Sen, 126
Asian Financial Crisis (AFC), 51, 52, 81, 85, 158

baby-boomers, 8, 126
basic public housing, 23
British National Health Service, 127

capital–labor rate, 92
city-state, 1
class inequality, 46
Community Silver Trust (CST), 114, 129, 131
co-payment policy, 127

co-payment scheme, 10
cost-of-living index, 19
CPF contribution rate, 60, 61, 64, 65, 70, 150
CPF salary ceiling, 60, 62–65, 69, 70

debt service ratios, 159
domestic human capital, 77, 78, 81, 91, 99, 100
domestic labor force, 78, 99

economic competitiveness, 7, 40
economic restructuring, 16, 21
Economic Review Committees (ERCs), 21
Economic Strategic Committee (ESC), 102
education costs, 23
educational landscape, 39
eldercare framework, 10
eldercare services, 128–130
ElderShield, 129
employability of older workers, 56
Employment Passes, 16, 17
entry-level public housing, 22
export competitiveness, 6, 91, 93

176 *Index*

fair consideration framework, 8
financial security arrangement, 11
financial transfers, 10
Foreign Domestic Worker Grant (FDWG), 114
foreign human capital, 91
foreign labor, 58, 78, 81, 83, 89–92, 95, 99, 100, 106
foreign wage rate, 95
foreign workers' levies, 16

Gifted Education Programme (GEP), 29, 30, 35
Gini coefficient, 3, 128
Global Competitiveness Index (GCI), 32
globally competitive workforce, 28
guaranteed universal coverage, 117

HDB Resale Price Index, 134
health care spending, 23, 125
health equity, 127
health inequality, 120
high wage policy, 13, 14
"hollowing-out" effects, 78
home ownership rates, 161, 162
household income data, 58, 137
housing affordability, 10, 11, 137, 146, 151, 153, 155, 157–159
Housing and Development Board (HDB), 133, 134, 136, 137, 141, 145, 148, 150, 151, 155, 157, 159, 162
human capital of foreign workers, 79

income distribution, 7, 11, 128, 135, 137, 150, 157, 158, 161
income gap, 13, 42, 140
income inequality, 25, 40, 42

income replacement rate (IRR), 9, 60–68, 71–73
industrial competitiveness, 79
inequality of opportunity, 35
information gaps, 106–108
Integrated Programme (IP), 29, 30, 35
Intermediate and Long-term Care (ILTC), 114, 118, 122–124, 131
international competitiveness, 6, 13, 14, 17
International Students Assessment (PISA), 26

job displacement, 66, 67
Job Vacancy Rate, 53
John Rawl, 127

knowledge-based economy, 81, 91

labor force, 78–82, 85, 87, 89, 90, 97, 99
labor force participation, 9, 75
labor productivity, 17, 24, 52, 53, 90, 91
lease buyback scheme, 9
Lee Hsien Loong, 131
Lee Kuan Yew, 43, 111, 126, 127
life expectancy, 61, 111, 118, 129
local human capital, 81, 91, 100–102, 106
long-term care (LTC), 111–116, 123, 124
long-term unemployment, 56, 58
low productivity, 6, 14–16, 19, 20

Maintenance of Parents Act (MPA), 118
Medifund Silver, 118, 122

Medisave, MediShield, and Medifund (3M) model, 10, 11, 115, 117, 128, 129, 130
meritocracy, 4, 8, 43, 45
Minimum Sum (MS), 62, 72, 116
Minimum Wage Policy (MWP), 16
model, 10
Monthly Living Wage (MLW), 18, 19

2013 National Day Rally speech, 7, 11
National University of Singapore (NUS), 133, 160, 161
National Wages Council (NWC), 13
non-resident employment, 58, 81, 82, 84–88
non-resident labor, 80, 81, 82, 85, 89
normal technical education, 30

old age financial security, 9
optimal, inclusive, balanced, green and clean (OIBGC), 18, 19

primary market transactions, 161
Primary School Leaving Examination (PSLE), 29, 30, 35, 43, 44
Private Residential Price Index, 133
productivity upgrading, 21
professionals, managers, and technicians (PMETs), 21
Progressive Wage Model (PWM), 6, 7
Programme for International Students Assessment (PISA), 26, 32–37
Public Housing Affordability, 10
public housing stock, 163
public housing system, 10, 161

Reformed Workfare Income Supplement (RWIS), 18
relative mobility, 43, 44

relative productivity, 6
Resale Price Index, 133, 134
resident employment, 82, 83, 85
retirement adequacy, 23, 24, 51, 59, 60, 63, 64, 66, 68–72, 74–76, 163

secondary public housing, 133
share of unemployment, 53, 55, 56
Singapore Perspectives, 3
Singapore Residential Price Index (SRPI), 133, 137, 143, 145, 160
Singapore-First Policy (SFP), 17
Small and Medium Enterprises (SMEs), 20, 21
social contract, 7
social inequality, 1
social mobility in Singapore, 45, 46
social welfare spending, 23
socioeconomic status (SES), 33, 34, 35, 44
Special Employment Credit (SEC), 75
steady-state growth rate, 96–98
structural unemployment, 58, 78
subject-based banding, 29

targeted special transfers, 16
teacher–pupil ratio, 23
tertiary education, 30, 31, 37, 40, 41, 70
three-sector general equilibrium model, 80, 95, 96
total factor productivity (TFP), 78
Total Fertility Rate (TFR), 129, 162, 163

unit business costs, 16
Unit Business Costs (UBC), 19, 20
Universal health access, 23
urban poverty, 5
Urban Redevelopment Authority (URA), 133

Vocational and Industrial Training
   Board (VITB), 31
vocational education, 31
voluntary welfare organizations
   (VWOs), 112–114, 118, 124, 125,
   130, 131

wage competitiveness, 70, 71
wage depression link, 58
wage growth, 7, 13, 60, 64, 66, 68, 70, 71
wage inequality, 101
wage stagnation, 3, 24
Wages–Productivity–Competitiveness
   (WPC), 14, 22
Workfare Income Supplement (WIS),
   15, 23
World Competitiveness Yearbook,
   125
World Economic Forum (WEF), 32,
   105

Printed in Great Britain
by Amazon